PLEDGING ALLEGIANCE

PLEDGING ALLEGIANCE

Learning Nationalism at the El Paso–Juárez Border

Susan J. Rippberger
Kathleen A. Staudt

RoutledgeFalmer   NEW YORK AND LONDON

Published in 2003 by
RoutledgeFalmer
29 West 35th Street
New York, New York 10001
www.routledge-ny.com

Published in Great Britain by
RoutledgeFalmer
11 New Fetter Lane
London EC4P 4EE
www.routledgefalmer.com

RoutledgeFalmer is an imprint of the Taylor & Francis Group.

10 9 8 7 6 5 4 3 2 1

Library of Congress Cataloging-in-Publication Data

Rippberger, Susan J.
    Pledging allegiance : learning nationalism at the El Paso-Juárez border / Susan J. Rippberger, Kathleen A. Staudt.
        p. cm.
    Includes bibliographical references and index.
    ISBN 0–415–93490–7 — ISBN 0–415–93491–5 (pbk.)
        1. Nationalism and education—Texas—El Paso—Cross-cultural studies.
    2. Nationalism and education—Mexico—Ciudad Juárez—Cross-cultural studies.
    3. Civics—Study and teaching (Elementary)—Cross-cultural studies. 4. Education, Bilingual—Cross-cultural studies. I. Staudt, Kathleen A. II. Title.

LC90.T4 R56 2002
372.83'2'0976496—dc21   2002069728

FOR SARA ÁNGEL
AND
FOR MOSI AND ASHA

CONTENTS

FOREWORD

Carlos Vélez-Ibáñez

The border region of Mexico and the United States has always been a remarkable setting for demographic, economic, social, cultural, and institutional change. It has been the site of confrontations of many sorts between the two nations—from the Mexican-American War to the daily battles suffered by Mexicans crossing the border seeking better sources of livelihood for themselves and their families. It has also been the site for many cross-border relations, often untold cooperative efforts, and mutuality between institutions often found only among families rather than between communities and nations.

The border is also a place for dynamic syncretism of culture, language, social relations, and the formation of special nexuses that individuals develop "in-between" nations such as cross-border households and networks of economic activities—formal and informal as well as underground. Yet, all of these characteristics are embedded in "localized" cultural practices and expectations influenced by a border reality. Even cultural identity is manipulated in times of stress, such as pretending not to speak English well to a border patrol officer in order to obfuscate perfect English that would give a person away as a practiced undocumented resident while using a temporary visit visa as the crossing document. Sometimes various legerdemains are used, such as crossing into Mexico transporting hidden bottles of perfume to sell without paying duties. Their odor is masked by the accumulated smells of decomposing, partially eaten burritos purposively laid out on the dashboard of the entering automobile. These are local cultural strategies embedded in myriad border practices and dynamics as I have written about elsewhere (Vélez-Ibáñez 1996).

Nevertheless, while the border is a place where nations, peoples, and cultures meet in this manner, the border also separates, keeps inequalities well honed, and ensures that ecologies are unbalanced. In general, borders are the places where respective nation-states, especially in the case of Mexico and the United States, focus special attention on national identity and often accentuate national locality and geography in order to deal with the many paradoxes that occur in which nationality is often not the practiced reference for daily intercourse.

Pledging Allegiance: Learning Nationalism at the El Paso–Juárez Border by Susan J. Rippberger and Kathleen A. Staudt is an outstanding contribution that gives us insights into the manner in which each respective state develops educational practices that seek to develop citizenship boundaries around often much more mutable practices and realities. Rippberger and Staudt illustrate how elementary school pupils on each side of the often-crossed border are located in learning environments in which nationalistic values and historical references create an important platform for the acquisition of citizenship and identity. What the authors show with great insight is that such learning is accomplished through culturally variable means in which their respective pedagogies accentuate certain metavalues in comparison to the other. That is, the "citizenship training embedded in classroom organization, management strategies, and personal relationships between teacher and students" is quite different culturally one from the other (6).

Yet the authors point out that such metavalues are linked to the historical realities of the border region itself. For Mexicans, the border is a daily reminder of something created very recently in the aftermath of war, and it is a tale told and repeated in the curriculum to accentuate a national feeling of patriotism and loyalty to nation and honor. In a most interesting manner, defeat at the hands of the United States in the nineteenth century and territorial loss have provided Mexican nationalism with the continued impetus for national identity and an opportunity to rationalize defeat as the basis for greater loyalty to the symbols, practices, and accentuated nationalistic rituals of the Mexican nation-state. In comparing responses on questionnaires on nationalism, the authors cite one Mexican respondent as stating: "We have it and you don't" (69) and the authors conclude that Mexicans use affective language much more than do Americans—language that personalizes the relationship between the citizen and the state such as the possessive forms "my," "her," and so on.

On the El Paso side of the border, more diverse definitions of citizenship are articulated with use of symbols and attention to patriotism much less than on the Juárez side but strongly associated with a conservative government administration and international power (69). The authors show that this characteristic is made possible by the manifestation of U.S. political dominance, superiority in wealth, and the gross differences in material resources expressed on a daily basis between the two countries. Such conspicuous difference makes nationalism on the U.S. side a rather unimportant issue since its expression is displayed in so many other forms.

There are many features in *Pledging Allegiance: Learning Nationalism at the El Paso–Juárez Border* that contribute profoundly to our understanding of the manner in which a sense of nationality is transmitted in each national context. But among the most important is the way in which the authors systematically explain how the pedagogy used by the elementary schools in relation to national values is localized in underlying local cultural practices, that is, in light of the often cited "transnational" literature that emphasizes nonlocalized cultural learning. This work clearly shows that the very process used to teach "love of country" in Mexican elementary schools is embedded in activities in which networks of reciprocal obligations and responsibilities operate as the central mechanisms that define classroom responsibilities, cooperative behavior, self-reliance, and the sharing of duties. Emotively associated with simultaneity, spontaneity, and "polychronic" use of time that lacks lineality, academic and civic learning are in fact reflective of learned cultural expectations by which many Mexican extended familial networks operate in difficult economic and ecological circumstances, such as those that exist in border cities. Tied to a Piagetian rationale, Mexican elementary schools operate to reinforce expectations of familial and community networks of mutual trust (*confianza*) and reciprocal obligations inculcated through dense relations between teachers and students expressed emotively, verbally, and by touch. Thus national, regional, local, and household levels are linked in a series of analogous cultural practices and expectations that are well understood and taken as "natural."

The El Paso schools also attempt to inculcate national values that are embedded in the pedagogy of instruction. The use of time is in fact "monochromic" time in which stress is placed on lineality—on single tasks, individual responsibility for work, self-reliance, stratified obligations based on status and ascribed roles, and in which a great deal of importance is given to individuality and independence but within highly controlled and ascribed group activities.

If it were possible to encapsulate the most salient characteristic of each approach, it would be that, in the Mexican case, each pupil learns and is made self-reliant by membership and participation in flexibly organized group activities. In the U.S. case, each pupil participates in highly conforming group activities in order to become self-reliant within the confines of group expectations. There seems to be much more of a factory approach in the latter than in the former case.

Linguistically, the authors describe a bilingual context on both sides of the border. The necessity of speaking both languages is a requirement that emerges from the daily commerce and trade, frequent work crossings, and cross-border familial and social relations that are omnipresent. The schools reflect this reality with bilingual and ESL instruction in one form or another constituting the predominant pedagogy in El Paso and English as a Second Language given a high priority in Juárez. However, the educational approaches of each reflect national approaches to the issue of language learning with both Mexican and U.S. educational institutions geared for language assimilation of Spanish in the former and English in the latter. As the

authors point out, these practices are reflective of national assimila-
tionist policies that are often disengaged from the reality of the border
region.

*Pledging Allegiance: Learning Nationalism at the El Paso–Juárez
Border* is a crucial work that both informs about the current issues and
sets the stage for continued discussion of the roles of culture and educational institutions, nationality and citizenship, and border and local
identities. In fact, the authors have also implicitly set the stage for their
next book. Since over 80 percent of the El Paso school district's students are of Mexican origin and since a very large percentage of teachers are also born in Mexico or in the United States of Mexican origin,
further examination is critical to the manner in which the cultural
funds of knowledge and expectations carried from household and community articulate with those expected U.S. national referents of the
U.S. classroom. Such an examination, based on the type of systematic
and thorough multidimensional research accomplished by the authors
and reported in this fine work, has yet to be undertaken.

PREFACE

Susan J. Rippberger and Kathleen A. Staudt

We have many people to thank for *Pledging Allegiance,* a long-term project whose seeds were planted as far back as 1994. This research originated during Kathy Staudt's participation in a faculty development institute at the East-West Center of the University of Hawai'i. There she met Dana Davidson and Joseph Tobin, two of the three authors (the other, David Wu) based at the University of Hawai'i who wrote *Preschool in Three Cultures,* based on research and a video that focused on China, Japan, and the United States. This work inspired Kathy to pursue similar research at the U.S.–Mexico border. The research design has changed considerably given our interest in public schools, civics, and bilingual education. In the earliest stages of our work, Davidson and Tobin shared many insights and encouraged more research of this kind. We thank them for their encouragement and guidance.

In the fall of 1994, a group of border researchers convened to discuss the possible directions of such research. Among those who brainstormed with us, we acknowledge and thank Rodolfo Rincones, then evaluation director at the El Paso Independent School District and now our colleague and associate professor at the University of Texas at El Paso, and Beatriz Calvo Pontón, then researcher in anthropology and education at the Universidad Autónoma de Ciudad Juárez, now dean of the Departamento de Educación y Desarrollo Humano,

Universidad Iberoamericana, A.C., Mexico City. Kathy's former student, Carlos Chacon, was involved in early stages of the work. Although he passed on at a young age—a tragic loss of brilliance, creativity, and commitment—we acknowledge him and dedicate our video to him and to his memory.

Doing research in public schools is a potential logistical nightmare. We thank the "bureaucracy" for making it possible, but especially the principals, school directors, and teachers in both Juárez and El Paso. They grounded us in their campus settings. Many campus leaders and teachers are heroines and heroes, although often unsung.

While Kathy came up with the topic, and invited Susan into the research when she first moved to El Paso in 1995, this became a co-researched, co-written, co-analyzed book, in which we both spent long hours in complementary work with complementary styles. Susan, once a bilingual teacher in public schools in California, and a researcher in Mexico, focused primarily on the Juárez side of the research. Kathy, a border researcher, focused on the El Paso side.

Our first and most valuable associate in Juárez was Gabriela Flores Balbuena, director of Special Projects in Education for the Northern Zone of Chihuahua, with offices in Juárez. Licenciada Flores Balbuena was instrumental in our work, providing entry into schools, classrooms, school systems, archives, and state offices. She gave us permission for visiting classrooms and doing research, and introduced us to teachers and local and state level administrators in Mexico. She went on research trips with us, and provided her understanding and analysis of our observations on Mexican schooling. She made sure we were invited to every computer lab inauguration in Juárez and in the outlying towns. Her diligence and thoughtful camaraderie helped make our research an enjoyable endeavor. We also thank Octavio Márquez (whom Gabriela married during our research), and Margarita Gallegos, who worked in Special Projects, for their kind guidance, rigorous support, and thoughtful perspectives.

Our methodology was complicated and comprehensive. The videotaping was an adventure, filmed at different times by Kathy Staudt, Susan Rippberger, and Sara Guerrero-Rippberger. Sara edited twenty-five hours of video to create an ordered, meaningful forty-five-minute version, helping us organize the themes portrayed in the video. This was the video that we showed to various audiences for initial feedback. We thank many others who helped us at this stage, Kathy Rogers, then director of news and publications, UTEP, David Flores, then coordinator of photography and video production, UTEP, who are now married to each other and have their own video creation consultant business. We thank also Ralph Escandon, for help with the narration and recording equipment, Everardo Hernández and Glen González, offering conscientious and friendly assistance during the filming and narration at KCOS Public TV, based at UTEP. Mónica Contreras narrated the video in both its English and Spanish versions. She exemplifies the binational and bilingual qualities of *fronterizas* (borderlanders) with multiple skills and commitments.

Susan also thanks others in her life who helped make this possible: To her family in California, who have always been supportive, and to her brothers and sister, David, Hope, Joel, Mark, Donny, and Matthew, that are always proud of their sister. To her mom, Irene Mae Moody Rippberger, and her dad, Donald Raymond Rippberger, who never failed to provide spiritual and moral support, constant love, patience, and guidance through life, and encouragement to fulfill her aspirations and live up to her ideals. To her mother-in-law in Cuernavaca, Morelos, Mexico, Guadalupe Navarro de Guerrero, for her support and love, and her sisters-in-law, Coqui, Clara, Angélica, and Mara, who welcomed her warmly and took her into their professional lives, sharing their insights on Mexican education. To Conchita Franco, educational researcher, in Chihuahua, and her daughter, Nora López, engineer and activist, who provided so much advice and logistical help with the research. And in El Paso, she thanks Nita Qualtrough, who provided constant spiritual support during the writing process that buoyed her, making long hours of writing a joy and an adventure. To Liz Amato, bilingual teacher, born in Mexico, who shared her understanding of popular culture in El Paso, and her home in Zacatecas, Mexico. And to Alejandra Hurtado for helping to put together the tedious but necessary job of the book's bibliography.

Susan offers heartfelt gratitude to Kathy for guidance and mentoring throughout the project, a rigorous scholar, acknowledged in her own field, political science, and in others as well, such as education and anthropology. Kathy is forever grateful for the opportunity to work with Susan, her colleague and dear friend, a friendship strengthened in the mostly exciting but also stressful collaborative research and writing process. Although Kathy was trained in positivist thinking (despite calling herself a "closet anthropologist" in a preface from nearly two decades ago), she has learned enormously from *maestra* Susan and her deep knowledge of ethnography in her heart, soul, and mind.

Finally, and most important, we offer this book to our children who make us realize just how crucial teachers and campus cultures are for learning and growing into healthy adulthood—a healthiness for both themselves individually and the wider society. Kathy thanks Mosi, first-born son, and Asha, life and hope, precious people with names that have meanings in multiple languages (Swahili and Hindi). Susan sends love and appreciation to Sara Ángel, her daughter, for inspiration, encouragement, and for very creative and critical analysis all along the way, including her suggestion for the title, *Pledging Allegiance*.

We both thank all those with whom we had conversations on education, culture, nationalism, and the border, and more generally, our larger borderland community, the *fronterizas* and *fronterizos*, for their creative construction of an insightful region—a region that promises to hold clues for the future of both the United States and Mexico.

CHAPTER 1

Introduction: Public Schools
and Nationalism

Josefina stands facing the front wall of her bilingual classroom, hand over
her heart, trying to mouth the words of the Pledge of Allegiance to the
principal's voice flooding into the room over the loudspeaker.
(El Paso bilingual second grade classroom)

For the Josefinas, Antonios, Erikas, Davids, and the millions of other
children in U.S. classrooms, this ritual is repeated daily and yearly
throughout elementary school and sometimes into middle and high
school. For children in Mexico the flag ceremony is quite different:
each Monday, the whole school gathers in the courtyard for an elabo-
rate flag ceremony that includes the Mexican pledge, the national
anthem, and a flag bearer with color guards and often a trumpet corps.
Looking back on our own experiences, we try to make sense of our
national identity, wondering about the connection between flag salutes
in school and responsibility for our country. As researchers, we wonder
what it is that students really are learning when they pledge allegiance
to their flag and country, and what the connection might be between
learning national values and practicing them.

The border is a unique setting to observe national and cultural values in education, juxtaposing differences between the United States
and Mexico in the El Paso and Juárez metropolitan area. Each year the

U.S. government counts 47 million crossers going north or south across international bridges to shop, visit relatives and friends, go to work, and attend school.[1] Signs on roads and freeways warn the southbound crossers against bringing guns into Mexico, while U.S. border agents watch entrants carefully for undocumented people and commerce.

In this mix of nationalities and languages, education attempts to teach children country-specific nationalism. Through curricula on history, civics, social studies, holidays, and cultural celebrations, children receive both explicit and subtle messages about what it means to be "American" or "Mexican." At the same time, however, the larger society and economic community train children to function in the mix of cultures on both sides.

The official version of nationalism found in textbooks competes with border transnationalism, summarized in the words of a Mexican second grade teacher:

> Our textbooks teach children that we have a unified nation, symbolized by one flag and one system of money for the whole country. But that's just not true. Here we see two flags daily [the Mexican and U.S.] and we use two systems of money [pesos and dollars].[2]

Public schools attempt to reinforce cultural and national values to create "good" citizens with much more than flag rituals. But what are good citizens? To what values do students pledge their allegiance? Questions such as these guide our thinking on how nations and nationalities are defined within a border area. Citizenship and nationalism are complex, involving both identity and civic virtues that are taught in and out of school. Concepts of citizenship, democracy, and

---

1. See Kathleen Staudt and Randy Capps, "Con La Ayuda de Dios? El Pasoans Manage the 1996 Immigration and Welfare Reforms," report for the Center for Immigration Research, University of Houston, with support from the Ford Foundation, forthcoming in *Living in the Interim: Immigrant Communities and Welfare "Reform" in North America,* ed. Ana Aparicio, Phil Kretsedemas, and Kalyani Rai (Westport, Conn.: Greenwood).

2. Many on the border carry both dollars and pesos; Juárez businesses accept both dollars and pesos, El Paso businesses take only dollars.

multiculturalism are interrelated and affect education and the way we shape a nation's civic consciousness.[3] If we do not include multiculturalism in nationalism, then we exclude major segments of society in both Mexico and the United States, and we revert to previous melting pot agendas that focused on an imaginary "oneness" in an attempt to assimilate diverse people to a European-centered mold.

The El Paso–Ciudad Juárez[4] border metroplex, in the states of Texas and Chihuahua, respectively is a binational area of approximately 2 million people. When we conducted this study, El Paso was the seventeenth-largest city in the United States, with a population of approximately 700,000, while Juárez, Mexico's fifth-largest city, had a population estimated at 1.5 million. At this border, the so-called developed world joins the less-developed world, offering a spotlight on education and its effects on both countries. Dividing the two cities is the río Bravo, as it is called in Mexico, or the Rio Grande to English speakers in the United States. It was not until the 1964 Chamizal Agreement between the United States and Mexico that the riverbed was cemented to stop its natural meandering in favor of a fixed political boundary. We found this a perfect place to study the pedagogy of nationalism.

A major port of entry, El Paso/Juárez shares a river, desert, and mountain range, as well as environmental and health problems. The two cities are brought even closer because each is isolated geographically from other cities in their own countries. National and cultural symbols permeate not only schools but also streets. Walking through neighborhoods in Juárez and El Paso, one sees murals of the Virgin of Guadalupe, the patron saint of Mexico. Children and families on both sides of the border celebrate Halloween and *día de los muertos,* and, at Christmas, the *posadas* and *reyes magos.*[5] Mexico commemorates a U.S. president, with a

---

3. See Carlos Alberto Torres, "Democracy, Education, and Multiculturalism: Dilemmas of Citizenship in a Global World," *Comparative Education Review* 42, no. 4 (1998): 421–47.

4. We use "Ciudad Juárez" (the formal name) and Juárez interchangeably.

5. Day of the Dead, celebrated on November 2, commemorating those who have gone before us, and Three Kings Day, celbrated on January 6, the Joseph and Mary peregrination.

statue of Abraham Lincoln on Avenida Lincoln in Juárez, while former Mexican dictator Porfirio Díaz has a street named after him in El Paso.

A huge Mexican flag, visible to residents on both sides of the border, was erected under President Zedillo's term (1994–2000). In El Paso, an electric-lit "lone star," visible to both sides,[6] shines each evening from the side of the Franklin Mountains (the continuation of the Rocky Mountains in the United States and the Sierra Madres in Mexico). An El Paso downtown bank illuminates red, white, and blue lights in the pattern of the stars and stripes on the façade of its building just blocks from the international border. At night, it would be difficult to determine where densely settled Juárez stops and El Paso begins, if it were not for the civic lighting.

Through the Juárez/El Paso portal comes America's largest immigrant population,[7] and, with it, a constant reaffirmation of Mexican culture as part of the U.S. culture. Juárez, too, is home to many migrants, who come, primarily from the interior of Mexico, for economic opportunity. According to Mexico's 1990 census, the decade in which we did our research, half of Juárez's residents were born outside the municipality.[8] The *maquiladora* industry boasts a 2000 labor force of 200,000, most of whom earn the official minimum wage equivalent of $20 to $40 (U.S.) weekly. Economic gaps between border communities are wide: per capita differences are ten to one and minimum wage gaps are five to one.[9]

---

6. The star on the Franklin Mountains can be lit by anyone for a modest fee paid to the El Paso Electric Company.

7. On borders, see Carlos Vélez-Ibañez, *Border Visions* (Tucson: University of Arizona Press, 1996); Oscar Martínez, *Border People* (Tucson: University of Arizona Press, 1994); Kathleen Staudt, *Free Trade? Informal Economies at the U.S.–Mexico Border* (Philadelphia: Temple University Press, 1998); Kathleen Staudt and David Spener, "The View from the Frontier: Theoretical Perspectives Undisciplined," in *The U.S.–Mexico Border: Transcending Divisions, Contesting Identities*, ed. David Spener and Kathleen Staudt (Boulder, Colo.: Lynne Rienner, 1998). For the last decade, INS reports show people of Mexican origin as the largest group of immigrants. After the 1986 Immigration Reform and Control Act authorized amnesty, Mexican-origin immigrants became the largest group to naturalize and acquire citizenship.

8. www.inegi.gob.mx

9. Staudt, *Free Trade?* chap. 3.

Photo by Susan Rippberger

Downtown El Paso.

As our nations merge through connected economies, popular culture, the Latin explosion, and diversity becoming mainstream, what becomes of conventional notions of nationalism? How do hierarchies of national values and customs get reordered? In this book, we examine the mix of national values and acculturation through everyday classroom settings in Juárez and El Paso. We look into how children are taught national values and what values they actually learn. This first chapter frames the study, describes central issues, and explains our specific field methods in understanding border education and national values. We describe specific schools in the region to illustrate the rich environmental and educational differences.

The following chapters describe the context and history of border education and present the basic themes that explain how children learn nationalism in school settings. What do societies value enough, both culturally and nationally, to teach children in schools? What meanings do everyday classroom dramas at the U.S.–Mexico border have for civic capacity at the border and for the heartlands of each country?

Four issues emerged as we investigated schools in Juárez and El Paso. First are the more obvious lessons on nationalism such as values programs, learning to vote, and flag salutes. How do border students and teachers respond to national values? Do they reject and/or reconstruct values, and with what strategies? The second issue concerns less obvious citizenship training embedded in classroom organization, management strategies, and personal relationships between teacher and students. How do schools turn children into "good" Mexican or U.S. citizens, or both—good binational citizens? The third issue is bilingualism and language use on the border. What do schools stress about cultural, linguistic, and national identities? What is the overlap between culture and nationality? The fourth, technology as a tool for both accountability and autonomy, poses a unique set of questions. What is the connection between technology in education and underlying issues of civics and nationality? What does the use of technology for accountability say about what we value nationally? These issues and questions frame our analysis of how children learn nationalism in Juárez and El Paso schools.

SCHOOLING ON THE BORDER

By analyzing binational education in El Paso and Juárez, we provide ways to understand the heritage of grandparents, parents, and children of the growing Latino population in the United States, soon to replace African Americans as the largest minority group. Together, they will form the majority of the new labor force by 2050.[10] Among Latinos, people of Mexican heritage numerically outnumber Puerto Ricans, Cubans, and others. In El Paso, over 80 percent of the population is of Mexican heritage. The border culture and history are part of U.S. culture and history, and they tell us of our multicultural makeup.

---

10. U.S. Department of Labor, *Futurework: Trends and Challenges for Work in the 21st Century* (Washington, D.C.: U.S. Department of Labor, 1999). Also see www.dol.gov/asp/futurework/report.

U.S. teachers and administrators must understand Mexican educational practices so students can learn more effectively. Mexican teachers would also benefit from understanding U.S. educational practices in a binational area. Diversity in teacher education is not just about acknowledging multiculturalism in the United States. It is also about using diverse teaching and learning strategies, based partly on who students are and how they learn. If Mexican students bring respect for teachers, reverence for the nation, or a reluctance to question those in authority to the classroom, for example, these "learned" civic behaviors are relevant for U.S. classroom practices. Understanding the U.S. emphasis on reading, language, and critical thinking might be important for Mexican policymakers in planning budgets for libraries and for purchase of other classroom books to supplement the official textbooks offered through the Secretaría de Educación Pública (SEP).[11]

In El Paso two languages are increasingly becoming the norm in classrooms, given the growing economic and social clout of the Latino population nationwide. About a quarter of resident El Paso children learn in bilingual classes, to help them make the transition from Spanish to English instruction. Two-way dual language, Spanish and English programs operate in several school districts. In Juárez, primary school children learn English as a Second Language (ESL) to provide them with added linguistic capacity for economic and social opportunities.

For more than a century, U.S. educational policies have Americanized immigrants to English just as Mexican policies tried to "Mexicanize" the hundreds of indigenous language speakers to Spanish. To deal with cultural diversity today, teachers in the United States and Mexico have been encouraged to value "multicultural" education, through required pre-service courses and in-service workshops. With multicultural approaches, students most commonly learn lessons about cultural celebrations and holidays and less commonly about racism, prejudice, and white privilege.[12] "Teaching for Diversity" has

---

11. Secretariat of Public Education.

12. See Ian F. Haney-Lopez, *White by Law: The Legal Construction of Race* (New York: New York University Press, 1996); Peter McLaren, "Unthinking Whiteness,

become the buzzword phrase that followed multicultural education. In the late 1980s a respect for cultural diversity and students' primary language in Mexico, too, was espoused along with national language unity.[13]

The border inspires reflection on difference, similarity, and blends of Mexican and U.S. educational practices. Borders have been called "in-between places,"[14] where people share common ground that goes beyond the land itself to include the exchange of ideas and practices. Nationalism may be weak at borders since people feel part of both nations, or it may be especially strong as people overemphasize differences to create a sense of national solidarity. Looking at the concept of nationalism at the border, we contrast different political versions of nationalisms in an area that shares an economic, social, and geographic environment.

For all the commonality that joins both sides of the border, ultimately the territorial line represents both the frontlines and limits of national sovereignty. The four main bridges that connect the two cities are busy night and day, transporting people over the river and six parallel chain link fences (at the downtown area) and past scores of U.S. and Mexican border patrol agents. Local radio stations give the approximate time for crossing the bridge by car as often as they give the weather (in both Celsius for Mexicans and Fahrenheit for Americans).

Rethinking Democracy; a Farewell to the Blonde Beast; towards a Revolutionary Multiculturalism," *Educational Foundations* (spring 1997): 1–29; *Rethinking Our Classrooms: Teaching for Equity and Justice* (Milwaukee: Rethinking Schools, 1996, or their website: www.rethinkingschools.org). The literature on multiculturalism is replete with books, articles, and even handbooks. Literature on "white privilege" belatedly joins this approach to add deeper dimensions.

13. Instituto de Investigación para el Desarrollo de la Educación, A.C. (IIDEAC), *Perfil de Formación de Maestros Primera Parte: Trayectoria y Prospectiva de la Modernización Educativa (1989–1994)*. Mexico, D.F.: Instituto de Proposiciones Estratégicas, A. C.,1992; Secretaría de Educación Pública (SEP), *Bats'i K'op, Lengua Tsotsil, Chiapas, primer ciclo*. México, D.F.: Comisión Nacional de los Libros de Texto Gratuitos, 1994.

14. Homi Bhabha. "Narrating the Nation," in *Nationalism*. ed. John Hutchison and Anthony D. Smith (New York: Oxford University Press, 1994); and Gloria Anzaldúa. *Borderlands: The New Mestiza=La Frontera* (San Francisco: Spinsters/Aunt Lute, 1987).

Learning nationalism on the border involves many issues: multiple ethnic groups,[15] two national systems of education, multiple languages, immigration, and the blurring of these seemingly separate issues. For example, in El Paso, where many of the school-aged children and their families are immigrants, bilingualism is the norm. Formal institutions include the Hispanic Chamber of Commerce, the Hispanic Women's Network, the Black Chamber of Commerce, the Korean Chamber of Commerce, and the Greater [Anglo] Chamber of Commerce.

While some Anglos are bilingual, others who are English-only speakers resent and resist this bilingual norm. Disgruntled letter writers to local newspapers complain about government workers speaking Spanish on the job or the preference for bilingual applicants in hiring and they wonder, "Is this America?"

Sociologist E. Bogardus, who wrote during the early 1900s, might agree; his words illustrate the contradictory and perhaps hegemonic notion people hold of language. He first implies that language is essential to one's identity, then he elevates English above other languages.

> When you strike at the language of a person, you strike at his feelings, his mother tongue, his childhood memories. The importance of English cannot be made too manifest. The value of English should be made so clear that all who do not know it should be stimulated to want to learn it.[16]

Sociolinguist E. Haugen's focus on language dominance sheds light on debates that center on English only (or Spanish only in Mexico) versus language pluralism,

> To choose any one vernacular as a norm means to favor the groups of people speaking that variety. It gives them prestige as norm-bearers and a head start in the race for power and position.[17]

---

15. Besides Mexican and Anglo (European American), other groups include Mexican American, American Mexican, Rarámuri, Tigua, African American, and Asian.

16. Emory S. Bogardus, *Essentials of Americanization* (Los Angeles: University of Southern California Press, 1923), 346.

17. E. Haugen, "Dialect, Language, and Nation," in *Sociolinguistics*, ed. J. B. Bride and Janet Holmes, (London: Penguin Books, 1972), 109.

Language and culture extend beyond patterns of everyday life to include shared understandings that shape social experiences and relationships.[18] Often cultures and languages of those in power are favored over others. But in a border situation where upper-middle-class Mexicans carry social and economic influence, and Spanish speakers outnumber English speakers, the status hierarchy of language is dismantled.

El Paso has a foreign-born population totaling approximately one quarter of its residents, most of them from Mexico. People who apply for citizenship encounter rules and regulations that put the meaning of citizenship into stark relief. "Naturalization," the term used by the Immigration and Naturalization Service (INS)[19] to signify the citizenship application process, is hardly easy or natural. To become naturalized is to undergo a five-year bureaucratic ordeal (with a flawless record, assuming it doesn't get lost) culminating in citizenship and English tests. The citizenship test, consisting of 100 questions, focuses on facts and details of U.S. history and government. This nationalist agenda is echoed in civics education in schools.

In its conventional meaning, civic education builds knowledge, skills, and the predisposition to engage in community and public affairs.[20] The strategies that educators use can range from lectures to experiential learning, but most are traditional, involving memorizing facts and details of U.S. government, history, economics, society, and geography. Civic education, or social studies, can also involve critical thinking and writing, debating, learning through experience, and group problem-solving approaches. Civic education is sometimes labeled

---

18. Sonia Alvarez, Evelina Dagnino, and Arturo Escobar, "Introduction: The Cultural and the Political in Latin American Social Movements," in *Cultures of Politics, Politics of Cultures: Re-visioning Latin American Social Movements* (Boulder, Colo.: Westview, 1998), 3. Also see Renato Rosaldo, *Culture and Truth* (Boston: Beacon Press, 1989), who differentiates between the fixed and static conceptualization of culture as museum-like, and culture as the everyday in a garage-sale model.

19. In Spanish, the acronym is SIN, for Servicio de Inmigración y Naturalización.

20. This definition draws on the National Assessment of Educational Progress (NAEP), *1998 Civics Report Card* (http://nced.ed.gov/nationsreportcard/).

service learning, democracy education, and/or citizenship training, but classroom management strategies that require obedience and passivity versus critical engagement are at the heart of civic education.[21]

METHODOLOGY AND THEORETICAL FRAME

To understand nationalism in education, we chose to focus on underlying assumptions, contradictions, and new possibilities in education.[22] Our work, based on definitions of education found in readings by authors such as Paulo Freire and Sonia Nieto,[23] celebrates individual differences, pluralist forms of democracy, and emancipatory educational practices. Such a theoretical perspective on education lends itself to qualitative research methods in which there is room for multiple voices and perspectives on civics and schooling. It also goes beyond describing current schooling and socialization, to exploring norms and expectations that underlie educational systems. Qualitative research

21. See Staudt, "Democracy Education for More than the Few" in *Developing Democratic Character in the Young*, ed. Roger Soder (San Francisco: Jossey-Bass, 2001); Robert Bellah et al., *Habits of the Heart* (New York: Harper & Row, 1985 and *The Good Society* (New York: Vintage, 1992); Robert Putman, "Bowling Alone: America's Declining Social Capital," *Journal of Democracy* 6 (1995): 1, and *Bowling Alone: The Collapse and Revival of American Community* (New York: Simon & Schuster, 2000); National Commission on Civic Renewal, *A Nation of Spectators: How Civic Desengagement Weakens America and What We Can Do about It* (College Park, Md.: NCCR, n.d.). These writers draw on Alexis de Tocqueville, *Democracy in America*, based on his 1830s travel. See also Sidney Verba, Kay Schlozman, and Henry Brady, *Voice and Equality: Civic Volunteerism in American Politics* (Cambridge, Mass.: Harvard University Press, 1995).

22. For critical theory and phenomenological perspectives on educational research, see Cleo H. Cherryholmes, "Social Knowledge and Citizenship Education: Two Views of Truth and Criticism," *Curriculum Inquiry* 10 (1980): 115–41; Beatriz Calvo Pontón, *Educación Normal y Control Político* (México, D.F.: Centro de Investigaciones y Estudios Superiores en Antropología Social, 1989); José Ángel Pescador Osuna, *Aportaciones para la Modernización Educativo* (México, D.F.: Universidad Pedagógica Nacional, 1989).

23. Sonia Nieto, *Affirming Diversity: The Sociopolitical Context of Multicultural Education*, 2nd ed. (New York: Longman, 1996); Paulo Freire, *Pedagogy of the Oppressed*, rev. ed. (New York: Continuum, 1996).

offers a means for understanding a school's role in reinforcing national and cultural values, thus fitting children into adult life.

Working in a natural setting, observing and participating with those in our study, helped us to see what goes on in schools without imposing artificial research conditions. Going into schools, we worked with students, their parents, teachers, and administrators to appreciate the issues from their vantage points.[24] One objective was to advance our understanding of nationalism and to connect the separate disciplines of education, anthropology, and political science in new and intriguing ways. Another objective was not to generalize what we learned, but rather to share it with others who may find commonalities with their own situation and experiences as they teach or parent future citizens.

FIELDWORK AND OTHER METHODS

Following basic ethnographic methods of observation and participation, we got to know our schools, visiting frequently and engaging in conversations for a period of about five years. We developed a complementary support system with full collaboration from the university, public schools, and the administrative offices in both Juárez and El Paso. The binational nature of this study supplied us with rich experiences for interacting with Juárez colleagues. Living on the border, we were able to help organize a number of binational conferences, attend many others, and visit each other's schools frequently during our research. We attended important educational functions on either side of the border; we served on master's theses committees; and we spoke at graduate gatherings at the local Juárez university, Universidad Autónoma de Ciudad Juárez. Traveling for joint research projects with colleagues from Juárez gave us the opportunity to hear both their thoughts about our observations and their interpretations of what we saw.

---

24. For more information on qualitative research techniques, see Sharan B. Merriam, *Qualitative Research and Case Study Applications in Education* (San Francisco: Jossey-Bass, 1998); Michael Quinn Patton, *Qualitative Evaluation and Research Methods* (Newbury Park, Calif.: Sage Publications, 1990); and Harry F. Wolcott, *The Art of Fieldwork* (Walnut Creek, Calif.: AltaMira Press, 1995).

Photo by Susan Rippberger

Author Kathleen Staudt filming Juárez first grade class.

On our school visits, we filmed approximately twenty-five hours of classroom activities in El Paso and Juárez schools, during the mid-1990s, in order to analyze their content for national and cultural values. We concentrated on primary schools, focusing on cultural, national, and border similarities. We edited the video footage to about one hour in length, to show back to students and educators who were in the video in order to give them the opportunity to respond to what they saw in the video.[25] The educators, parents, and students who

---

25. On ethnographic literature, see Shirley Heath, *Ways with Words: Language, Life and Work in Communities in Classrooms.* (Cambridge: Cambridge University Press, 1983); George Spindler, ed., *Education and Cultural Process: Anthropological Approaches.* (Prospect Heights, Ill.: Waveland Press, 1987). Initial inspiration for this book came from a workshop and the book/video, Joseph Tobin, David Wu, and Dana Davidson, *Preschool in Three Cultures* (New Haven, Conn.: Yale University Press, 1989), in which the authors selected three preschools in urban areas of China, the United States, and Japan wherein they videotaped a "typical" day. They subsequently showed their video to audiences in all three countries, with the intention of learning culture through people's defense of and/or challenge to other cultural practices in education.

watched the video analyzed it with us, giving us insight into their unique perceptions.

Our next step was to edit the one-hour video to about forty-five minutes and add a narration, one version in English, another in Spanish. We showed the edited video to hundreds of educators and students from 1996 through 2000 in Juárez and El Paso. Prior to the video viewing and afterward we distributed questionnaires (in both languages) to spark dialogue about the video. The questionnaire asked the viewers' opinions about the purpose of schooling and the meaning of citizenship. This gave us a third layer of analysis to add to our own observations and the commentary of those who viewed themselves on the video, giving us a broader, deeper analysis involving many more schools, students, and educators.

In addition to observations and conversations with students and educators, we interviewed education officials, studied curricular materials, and attended school functions and school board meetings. We visited the SEP's state archives in the state capital, Chihuahua City, for information on education in the state and in Juárez. We also read in special library archives and traveled with parent activists to the state capitol, Austin, Texas. In Austin, parents rallied in support of increased funding for parental engagement. For several years, we clipped newspaper articles from *Diario de Juárez, Norte,* and the *El Paso Times,* for issues, trends, and perspectives in education on the border.

OUR SCHOOLS

Over a quarter of a million children attend public elementary and secondary schools in Juárez and El Paso. El Paso County has nine school districts; Juárez schools are under the administration of the SEP's Zona Norte.[26] We visited many of these schools, but videotaped in only five. In El Paso, we videotaped monolingual and bilingual public school classrooms in the low- and middle-income neighborhoods of Vilas and Schuster Elementary Schools. In Juárez, we went to three schools in low- and middle-income neighborhoods, one near the

---

26. Northern Zone.

downtown area, within walking distance of the border, the other two about fifteen minutes' driving distance from the border. Because El Paso and Juárez schools are different in many ways, we describe first their general characteristics, then describe each individually in detail.

EL PASO SCHOOLS

In El Paso we chose two schools, Vilas Elementary School, close to the border, and Schuster Elementary School, farther away. Both have bilingual classrooms with a maximum of fifteen students per classroom, set by school district policy at the time of our study. The state of Texas sets all class sizes, monolingual and bilingual for grades pre-kindergarten through third grade, at twenty-two per teacher. Fourth grade and up, classes had a cap of thirty-five students per teacher at the time of our research. Districts may lower these numbers, if they can afford to hire extra teachers.

The schools have libraries staffed by full-time librarians and an auditorium that can double as a cafeteria. Most classrooms have a TV and VCR and several computers. Lower grades sometimes have rest-rooms inside the classroom. The playground is usually an asphalted area to the side of or behind the school.

VILAS ELEMENTARY SCHOOL

Vilas School is near the downtown international bridge that crosses the Rio Grande and joins the city centers of Juárez and El Paso. Vilas, named after a New York migrant to the region who was elected to the El Paso School Board, sits in the Sunset Heights Historic District in a two-story building. During the Mexican Revolution of 1910, residents in this district watched the shooting in Juárez from their rooftops. Those who fled the revolution often settled in El Paso, some of them wealthy migrants who bought stately homes in Sunset Heights. A street named Porfirio Díaz runs through the center of this neighborhood. Sunset Heights is today a mix of old homes, large and small, some subdivided, others remodeled.

Vilas School has almost 100 percent Mexican-American students.

Photo by student in classroom

Kathleen Staudt with El Paso classroom.

All first grade classes are bilingual except for one monolingual English classroom. Other grade levels have both bilingual and monolingual classes. We videotaped in the monolingual classroom and in a bilingual first grade whose teacher is a native Spanish speaker, and who attended elementary school in Juárez. Typical of many interethnic families in El Paso, she had married an Anglo and adopted his Anglo surname. She taught content knowledge in Spanish while gradually introducing students to English through serious but enjoyable lessons.

Most students (96 percent) are categorized "economically disadvantaged," that is, they qualify for subsidized lunches based on low family income. At the time of our research, Vilas had approximately 15 percent immigrant students, the highest number for El Paso schools. Some students (often U.S. citizens living in Juárez) walked across the border each day for school. Teachers told us of higher student absenteeism on Mexican national holidays, and before Juárez changed its time to match daylight savings time in the United States, of sleepy students who occasionally arrived an hour early by mistake.

Classroom walls are filled with colorful posters, lists, and student work. Even walls in classroom restrooms have educational posters and charts. In some classrooms, bulletin boards feature a student of the month. These displays include photographs of the student, and student-drawn pictures of their hobbies, and dreams, for example, to become a ballet dancer or firefighter. By the end of the year, all students are rotated through this privilege. Prominent among classroom posters are lists of rules, including the "assertive discipline plan." Building on behaviorism, this plan rewards good behavior symbolically by listing those who exhibit "good" behavior on the chalkboard under a caricature of a happy face. Conversely, for "bad" behavior, teachers write students' names under a caricature of a sad face. In many schools, progressive penalties with consequences are in place: name on the board, check mark after the name, student referred to the principal's office, and, finally, the parent is notified. Allegedly this "plan" reinforces "good" citizenship, namely, following the rules.

SCHUSTER ELEMENTARY SCHOOL

Schuster School, in the northeast section of El Paso, is a set of one-story buildings in a "pod" formation with classrooms fanning out from a central location. Named after a local doctor, Schuster has over 80 percent of the students receiving government-subsidized lunches. The student population is about 75 percent Mexican American, 20 percent Anglo, and 5 percent African American.

Schuster's diversity reflects the surrounding neighborhood: working poor to middle income, with some families connected to one of El Paso's military bases. The closest base, Fort Bliss, is a historic border post that gained visibility as host to Patriot missiles used during the 1991 Gulf War in the analogous desert-like environment of the Middle East. The school takes "Patriots" for its nickname, and it has an image of the U.S. flag printed on its school T-shirts.

Schuster's Mission Statement reads: "The administration, faculty, and staff of Schuster will provide the students with: A safe, disciplined environment that is warm and caring, professional instruction and guidance, and adequate amounts of necessary materials to insure that, with the help of the community and their parents, they can all learn the basics, succeed in school, and achieve life's goals."[27] Schuster School was awarded the nationally competitive Blue Ribbon status, a prestigious award given to schools that go above and beyond what is expected for students and the community. The school has one bilingual classroom for each of the primary grades.

JUÁREZ SCHOOLS

We focused on schools in Juárez from three different neighborhoods, Benito Juárez, Nicolas Bravo, and Revolución. We specifically chose schools that might be comparable to El Paso schools in socioeconomic standing and in proximity to the border, taking into account the different meanings of class and income within each nation. The schools we visited each have a small auditorium, and one TV and VCR that all classrooms share. Two have small libraries. In Juárez most public elementary schools have two shifts, a morning and an afternoon. These shifts are actually two schools, each with its own director, set of teachers, and group of students. Revolución School even has a third shift in the evening. Cafeterias are not necessary since no meals are served during the half-day shifts. Each school has a refreshment stand, often run by parents, where children can purchase candies, drinks, and other snacks during recess.

BENITO JUÁREZ SCHOOL

Benito Juárez School is located several blocks from the international border in a densely settled downtown neighborhood called Bella Vista. It is so close to the international border that the El Paso downtown area is visible from the school grounds. In this residential area, homes are old, small, mostly owner-occupied, one- or two-bedroom cement

---

27. Campus Profiles, 1995–1996, El Paso Independent School District, Research and Evaluation.

Author Susan Rippberger with Juárez students.

houses. Small storefront businesses are mingled among the homes, where one room opens to the street, selling items like soft drinks, snacks, batteries, and hair products. On the corner is a *tortillería*.

Students at Benito Juárez School come from modest, but not economically desperate, backgrounds. Parents are part of the working class, employed in service and *maquiladora*[28] jobs where they earn the equivalent of $4 to $6 per day. Some children, who attend the afternoon shift, work during the morning washing car windows at stoplights, or selling gum. Teachers told us that children who attend the morning shift frequently come from more traditional and middle-class families, and they arrive at school cleaner, more cared for, and more often with homework done.

Long, one-story buildings house classrooms, forming the perime-

---

28. Export processing factory.

ter of the school around a central courtyard. The courtyard provides a natural gathering place for teachers, parents, and students, and it serves as a playground. At the corner is a concession stand with a big Coca-Cola sign where students can buy snacks during recess. The school was named after a beloved Mexican president, one of the first leaders with strongly indigenous features, so unlike the white Spanish administrators before Mexico's independence.

In Juárez we observed evidence of assertive discipline plans in many rooms. A Benito Juárez teacher told us that she wants her students to like school. She warns them that if they do not finish their work, they cannot go out for recess, and that if they do not get their name on the "happy face" side of the chalkboard, they will not get a piece of candy when they go home. These warnings are motivational rather than punitive, as students all go out to recess, work done or not, and all receive candy as they leave. She said she wants them to go home with a good feeling about school, so they return just as happy. She explained to us, "There are no bad kids, just some who have more trouble controlling themselves."

NICOLAS BRAVO SCHOOL

Nicolas Bravo School, named after a military leader, is located in a middle-class neighborhood about a mile from downtown Juárez. The neighborhood is mixed residential and business, with relatively new housing that resembles apartment-like condominiums. The Instituto de Fomento Nacional de Vivienda de Trabajadores (INFONAVIT)[29] builds these houses at affordable prices for the working class, based on workers' contributions to this fund.

As we arrived for our first visit, the principal greeted us warmly, inviting us into his office to talk about our project and see how he could work with us, chatting amicably over coffee and cookies. He told us that during the past year the school had celebrated its ninetieth anniversary, and he proudly showed us the school's ledger and attendance records

---

29. National Fund for Workers' Housing.

from 1905, handwritten in script. He also showed us the school's basketball trophy. We toured the school, first visiting the two original rooms that had been the school, which are still used as classrooms. As we walked through the central courtyard, there were groups of girls and boys playing basketball at the two hoops. The director explained that they were practicing for a citywide intramural basketball tournament.

Surrounding the courtyard were five long buildings, each with numerous classrooms. Stopping in classes, we noticed the assertive discipline on chalkboards here, too. The school has one of the larger school libraries in the city, with approximately 250 titles. Books are not checked out, but read in the library, common to many libraries in Mexico. The library holds four small bookcases, a librarian's desk, and three round study tables. The walls are brightly decorated with posters; one spells out the library rules: no candies, no throwing trash on the floor, and no loud talking. Another poster lists an appropriate grade level for each book in the library's collection.

CENTRO ESCOLAR REVOLUCIÓN

Revolution Educational Center is an impressive and beautifully constructed three-story building, and a historical landmark. However, it is in great need of repair. The school has hardwood floors and French doors in each classroom, but many of the windowpanes in the doors are cracked or missing and floors are decaying. The school has a large auditorium, with stained glass windows, a library, a music room, and approximately thirty classrooms. The play area, unlike most Juárez schools, is off to the side of the building. Beautiful, but wind-damaged, stained-glass windows serve as a skylight at the school's center, a small court area that has room for a large staircase and a walkway on either side. The stained-glass windows depict Benito Juárez, the first Mexican president of Native Mexican heritage; Miguel Hidalgo, the priest given credit for starting the Mexican independence movement; Cuauhtémoc, the last Aztec ruler; Francisco I. Madero, Mexico's first elected president after the thirty-one-year reign of Porfirio Díaz, and the symbol on the Mexican flag—an eagle on a cactus with a snake in its claw.

Centro Escolar Revolución.

The principal here, too, treated us graciously, giving us a tour of the school, taking us into classrooms to meet students and teachers. She told us about her teachers, all licensed to teach, and very responsible. She also mentioned that they would like to repair the stained glass, but repairs are estimated at the equivalent of 4,500 U.S. dollars. Scarce funds are used for repairing water fountains, restrooms, and other more immediate needs.

PREVIEW OF CHAPTERS

The following chapters detail the way children learn nationalism in a border context. Chapter 2 provides a context for the mixed history that ties El Paso and Juárez together. It looks into governmental and legislative changes in education that have made education more equitable and accessible. Chapters 3 through 6 highlight our findings on nationalistic training through explicit lessons like the flag salute, celebration of national holidays, and rewards for civic behavior. We also look at character education programs and the complex nature of values systems. Chapter 4 draws attention to the subtle ways we teach national and cultural values—in the way teachers manage and organize their classrooms, their lessons, and their students. We examine what it means to be a good citizen in a context of binational perceptions of space, time, and individuality. Chapter 5 deals with language, emphasizing the bilingual nature of the border. It explores the ideologies surrounding language use, bilingual education law, and current practices in schools. Chapter 6 considers the meanings and uses of educational technology for self-directed learning as well as systems of accountability and standards. It examines the connections between technology in education and civics. Finally, chapter 7 offers closing perspectives, suggesting civic education strategies for a more engaged binational citizenry.

CHAPTER 2

Contextualizing Nationalism and Education

Nuestra historia tiene periodos y procesos complejos que no es sencillo, ni aconsejable, simplificar en exceso. . . . El propósito de este libro es proporcionar información sobre nuestro pasado, y despertar en los niños gusto por la historia y amor por la patria. Crear una conciencia de identidad común entre todos los Mexicanos.[29] (From the foreword to the fourth grade history book put out by the Secretaría de Educación Pública[30])

Like the history described in the foreword to the Mexican textbook, the history of El Paso and Juárez is complex and learning about it should awaken an appreciation for national identity in both countries. A town that was once exclusively Mexican, Paso del Norte, was divided into two nations in the mid-1800s. The educational system of each country has since diverged, promoting different nationalistic agendas. Because of a common history, though, the two cities have a natural affiliation that they maintain in spite of their political division.

---

29. Our history has complex times and processes that are not easy, nor is it recommended, to oversimplify. . . . The purpose of this book is to give information about our past and awaken in children an appreciation for history and love of country. To create a consciousness of common identity among all Mexicans.

30. *Historia: Cuarto grado*, Comisión Nacional de los Libros de Texto Gratuitos, Secretaría de Educación Pública, 1996.

Education in Mexico and the United States has been used to strengthen national identity and unity, focusing on (and privileging) mainstream urban populations and an official language. Understanding the context of nationalism and education in El Paso and Juárez can help clarify current practices and beliefs in teaching nationalism. Given the decentralized nature of U.S. education, with governance at state and local levels, a peculiar kind of nationalism occurs in Texas, which was once an independent nation, and whose flag still waves proudly.

Mexico has historically concentrated authority over education with the Secretaría de Educación Pública (SEP) located in Mexico City. The SEP is a cabinet-level agency that mandates one curriculum throughout Mexico.[31] In the United States, the Department of Education, born in 1979, works in coordination with state and local levels of school governance. More recently, Mexico has attempted to decentralize education by shifting certain responsibility to the state level, while U.S. education has become more centralized indirectly through common standards,[32] standardized testing, legislative directives, and the use of common textbooks.

MEXICAN SCHOOLING/JUÁREZ SCHOOLING

The SEP has a direct influence on border schooling through teacher training programs, curricular content, and attitudes promoted through textbooks. From its inception, public education in Mexico was designed to assimilate the nation's multicultural population to an urban mestizo culture and economy. A SEP publication promoting its textbooks points out the direct connection between the government and

---

31. See Bradley A. Levinson, Douglas E. Foley, and Dorothy C. Holland, eds., *The Cultural Production of the Educated Person: Critical Ethnographies of Schooling and Local Practice* (Albany: State University of New York Press, 1996), for a discussion of the one national curriculum imposed on all communities (urban, rural, indigenous, etc.) in Mexico.

32. For a discussion on the rise and fall of educational standards in the United States, see Diane Ravitch, *National Standards in American Education.* Washington, D.C.: Brookings Institution Press, 1995.

the educational system, stating that education is the source of patriotism and democracy:

> La obra del gobierno se halla orientada por el interés de las mayorías. La
> tarea educativa no puede constituir excepción, sino todo lo contrario; a ella
> convergen los mejores fuerzas de nuestro patriotismo y de nuestra
> democracia.[33]

Standard histories of schooling usually emphasize its role as an agent for integrating society, increasing economic productivity, and enhancing social mobility for individuals. The SEP publication asserts: "*La paz de la escuela es la paz de México*,"[34] tightening the relationship between nationalism and schooling.

Education, in the area now called Mexico has gone through various stages in response to political and social changes: the Spanish invasion of indigenous communities, independence from Spain in the early 1800s, a revolution in the early 1900s, a socialist reform period in the 1930s and early 1940s, and, most recently, a "modernization" program initiated by the government. Not only curriculum but also attitudes toward teaching and learning have undergone significant change. The rationale for gymnastics in the early 1900s, for example, reveals an attitude toward children and their place in the nation. Gymnastics was described as useful for coordination and patriotism, and it included marches to discipline the body and team sports to correct laziness and promote the subordination of the self.[35] Expectations of children's roles have also changed with differing philosophical views on education and

---

33. The government focuses on the interests of the majorities. The work of education is not an exception; it's a place where our best efforts at patriotism and democracy meet.

34. A peaceful school is a peaceful Mexico, from the Secretaría de Educación Pública, *Los Libros de Texto Gratuitos y las Corrientes del Pensamiento Nacional Vol. II* (México, D.F. : Biblioteca del Consejo Nacional Técnico de la Educación, 1962), 16.

35. See Mary Kay Vaughan, *The State Education, and Social Class in Mexico (1880–1928)* DeKalb: Northern Illinois University Press, 1982); also Carlos Ornelas, *El Sistema Educativo Mexicano: La Transición del Fin de Siglo* (México, D.F.: Centro de Investigación y Docencia Económica, 1995).

childhood, moving from passivity and obedience to active and challenging learners. Over the years, school programs also have become less religious and more secular, emphasizing government authority and nationhood.

An increase of school building in urban areas followed Mexico's independence in 1821. Governments of the mid to late 1800s built schools and created study plans to support the new nation and meet the need to inculcate a common history. Public schooling typically comprised two to three years of rudimentary instruction in speaking, reading, and writing Spanish and learning elementary math. In the consolidation of the nationalist approach to education, Catholic schools were placed under the direction of the Ministry of Education, and later normal schools were created to help standardize instruction.

Until the Treaty of Guadalupe Hidalgo in 1848, El Paso and Juárez had a common history. Rarely studied in U.S. elementary schools, this story sheds light on the subtleties of the relationship between the two nations and lingering misgivings. The event is summarized in the fourth grade textbook on history put out by the SEP.[36] The book explains that the war with the United States came at a time of political disorganization and national debt within Mexico, and the desire of some Texans to become part of the United States. Confrontations over the southern border of Texas provided the United States with an opportunity to declare war on Mexico, whose territory it had wanted for a long time. The United States quickly invaded California and New Mexico (northern Mexico) and the port of Veracruz (southeastern Mexico). From there, "enemy" troops crossed into central Mexico.

The textbook sadly relates, "*No hubo victorias en esta guerra. Pero sí heroísmo y sacrificio.*"[37] U.S. troops occupied Mexico City for nine months, planting its flag in the capital, "*El día 14 [de septiembre de*

---

36. *Historia Cuarto Grado*, Comisión Nacional de los Libros de Texto Gratuitos, 116.

37. There were no victories in this war. But there was heroism and sacrifice.

1847] la Ciudad de México fue tomada y la bandera enemiga ondeó en el Palacio Nacional."[38] The narrative continues, "the consequences were disastrous. Mexico had to sign the Treaty of Guadalupe Hidalgo, losing New Mexico, Alta California, Texas, and part of the state of Tamaulipas, . . . receiving fifteen million pesos. Its territory was reduced by a little less than a half, but the war made Mexicans feel like never before, the need to be unified."

An activity suggested on the same page tells students to trace the before-and-after maps and calculate the amount of territory that Mexico lost, then discuss the consequences with classmates. One of these consequences, highlighted in the last sentence, *"la guerra hizo que los Mexicanos sintieran como nunca antes la necesidad de estar unidos,"*[39] explains poignantly the national government's perspective on maintaining national territorial unity. As Juárez students cross the border to attend school in El Paso, they see a huge graffiti painted in bright turquoise on the cemented bank of the río Bravo that speaks to the activity to consider the consequences of Mexico's loss of territory: "¡¡¡*Ya Basta*!!!" it reads, *"Que Saddam Hussein regrese Kuwait y que Bush ponga el ejemplo regresandonos nuestros estados Tejas, Nuevo México, Arizona, y California; los Mexicanos los reclamamos aunque nos cueste nuestra propia sangre."*[40]

A decade after the war, President Juárez would organize public schooling at all levels—primary, secondary, and professional training. The 1860s curriculum included morality, and the country's fundamental laws, clearly a civics agenda. The Ley Orgánica de Instrucción called for free obligatory elementary schooling for all, to improve society and promote democracy.

---

38. On the 14th of September, Mexico City was taken and the enemy flag flew over the seat of the government.

39. The war made Mexicans feel, like never before, the need to be unified.

40. Enough! May Saddam Hussein return Kuwait and may Bush set the example by returning our states, Texas, New Mexico, Arizona, and California; Mexicans will reclaim them even though it may cost us our own blood.

With an expansion of schooling between 1895 and 1910, literacy as well as citizenship training were more widely promoted. Moral education continued to support community and nation building: love of work, and respect for the law and authority. Children were taught obedience and sacrifice. An emphasis on morality instruction helped Mexicans focus on repressing bad habits, such as ignorance, laziness, lack of savings, lack of punctuality, and lack of cleanliness. Like morality instruction today, it is often easier to make disenfranchised people responsible for their own problems than to reform structural problems that cause poverty and its effects.

By 1919, Juárez was still a rural frontier, but one of the largest towns in the state of Chihuahua. Of Chihuahua's 330,000 people, Juárez had 9,000 inhabitants and over 25 percent of the state's households. Eleven of the state's 225 schools were located in Juárez.[41]

It was in this context that José Vasconcelos became the first minister of education (1922–1934). During this reform era, elementary education was expanded to six years, and an emphasis was placed on moral citizenship through education. Specific educational goals included a love of country, and the ability to contribute to its progress, developing a physical, artistic, and moral sense, and preparing to enter the workforce. Vasconcelos saw the function of education as cultural, ideological, and economic, involving the formation of citizens, the development of the nation, and the promotion of democracy. To reach rural populations, the SEP established schools as community centers, offering elementary schooling as well as adult education classes. It was during this era that Boy Scout troops[42] were initiated to instill patriotic citizenship, trust, and cooperation in children.

Moving to secularize education, the SEP introduced a new national school calendar in 1925. The calendar was an attempt to institutionalize patriotic celebrations, replacing traditional Catholic reli-

---

41. Ponce de Leon, José María, *Anuario Estadístico del Estado de Chihuahua, Año 1910*, Chihuahua, 1910.

42. A concept borrowed from the United States open to both girls and boys in Mexico. The words *Boy Scouts* are not translated into Spanish.

gious holy days and church activities. Sixty days were dedicated to representations of civics and nation. Patriotic observations included births and deaths of national heroes, Mexican independence day, the battle of Puebla, and the beginning of the Mexican revolution, among others. Also on this calendar are significant dates that are largely invisible in the United States, such as April 21, 1914, the defense of Veracruz against the North American invasion, and March 18, 1938, added later, the anniversary of the expropriation of foreign oil companies.

Socialist reforms in the 1930s brought changes in education, focusing on culture and technical training, making education more practical and democratic. Social service was initiated, requiring students in upper grades and at the university to volunteer service to the community in their field. At least philosophically, schooling attempted to be more in tune with children's needs, encouraging them to actively participate and reflect on what they were learning.[43]

Textbooks presented free from the SEP also supported a unified nation. It was Torres Bodet, minister of public education from 1943 to 1949, who initiated free textbooks to be used uniformly throughout the nation. These books, written, published, and distributed by the SEP, ensured that one version of the nation's history was read by every student in the country. The SEP presents their textbooks as free, obligatory, patriotic, just, and indispensable. They explain that the books are *patriotic* because of their message of national unity and love for the republic, *just* in serving all children equally, and *indispensable* because they are to be used as a textbook and a reference book. According to the SEP's vision of education, the free textbooks are designed make children happy, and awaken in them the desire to be useful. Children are taught to revere these special books: to cover them so they last, write in them only when they are supposed to, wash their hands before they use them, put them away carefully, and not use them to sit on.[44]

---

43. In practice, though, education still relies heavily on rote learning.

44. Secretaría de Educación Pública, *Los Libros de Texto Gratuitos y las Corrientes del Pensamiento Nacional, Vol. II* (México, D.F.: Biblioteca del Consejo National Técnico de la Educación, 1962).

Since the 1940s, the SEP has continued to produce and distribute free textbooks to students in elementary schools, grades one through six.

Building on a vision where children take a more active part in their education, 1960s and 1970s studies focused on scientific methods for acquiring knowledge, and understanding daily life. The primary curriculum promoted critical and creative thought in students, and it sought to develop the capacity for abstract reasoning. Philosophy on teaching methods continued to change too, from dictation and memorization to observing, investigating, establishing cause-and-effect relationships, applying knowledge to resolve problems, serving others, fulfilling obligations, and demanding one's rights.

More recently, in the 1990s, the government has sought to transform education to promote social and economic modernization, with its Plan Nacional de Desarrollo[45] to improve the quality of national education for national development. Its goals, broad and vague, are to improve schooling, strengthen teacher qualifications, decentralize education, and encourage social participation, emphasizing technology and science in this process.[46] Without funding, though, the broad goals remain lofty ideals.

Under modernization, some of the financial responsibility for education was transferred from the nation's capital to state governments; the federal government retained control of the curriculum, programs, evaluation, and textbook publication. From the grand objectives for national modernization came specific educational modernization objectives that built on previous eras. These goals, a combination of humanistic and economic ideals, included human development without discrimination, national unity through Spanish, a respect for cultural pluralism, and the development of scientific knowledge, critical analysis, and the creation of international solidarity.

From 1910 to 1998, the growth rate of Juárez was explosive, increasing by more than 6,000 percent. Juárez, which had eleven

---

45. National Development Plan.

46. *Educación Básica: Secundaria Plan y Programas de Estudio* (México, D.F.: Secretaría de Educación Pública, 1993).

schools in 1910, now has more than 50 percent of all the schools in the state of Chihuahua.[47] One of the schools we observed was established during the reform era of the Cárdenas presidency, Centro Escolar Revolución in Juárez. Changes that this school has gone through illustrate some of the changes in education during the last thirty years. In talking with the director of the school, ex-students, and parents of those who have attended Revolución School we caught a glimpse of the sense of history, community, and solidarity that they had, and the connections they made between place and identity.

Revolución School was built as a showpiece educational center in 1939, under the presidency of Lázaro Cárdenas. President Cárdenas attended the inaugural ceremony, indicating the significance of the school and the town to the nation's development. The director of the school told us of a ninety-four-year-old woman who had children, grandchildren, and great grandchildren attend Revolución School. She loves to tell the story of President Cárdenas, who, touring the school, slipped and fell as he passed by the school's fountain and reflecting pool, getting himself wet. With grace and dignity, she relates, he picked himself up and continued the tour.

The school is located in an older downtown portion of the city, once a quiet residential area but now in decline. Many of the older homes have been converted to store fronts selling everything from household items to car parts and contraband designer clothing. The director told us that only eight original families still live in the immediate area and have children or grandchildren who attend Revolución School. Families are moving now to the newer areas away from the city center.

Two alumni, now school teachers themselves, reminisce about the school they attended thirty years before. This was the "original" Juárez, they told me, a neighborhood called Barrio Chaveña, after the Chaveña family remembered for their lovely daughters. On weekends they would meet with friends from school at the fountain behind the

---

47. INEGI, 1998, and Ponce de Leon, 1910.

school to splash and cool off during the hot summer months. One still lives in the area, the other had moved with his family to the more modern part of town.

We spoke with the *directora* of the Revolución School, who had been at the school thirty-five years, the last twelve years as the director.[48] Prior to that, she had worked twenty-three years off and on teaching, as she raised a family. Her own mother had finished primary school at Revolución, so she had a deep sense of personal history tied to the school.

We asked her to tell us about daily activities in the school twenty to thirty years ago. In those days, she explained, there was a lot more parental support, and the teachers were stricter. The school had about 1,400 students, three or four classes at each grade level, and up to fifty students per classroom. Since there were so many students and such a small patio, the director at the time had to create two recesses, one for the first three grades, the other for the older children.

Teachers had children in class all day, beginning at 9:00 A.M. with a lunch break from 1:00 P.M. to 3:00 P.M., and an afternoon session from 3:00 P.M. to 5:00 P.M. Mothers would meet their children at the school gate and walk them home, talking to them about their lessons. Since students spent most of the day at school, teachers had more time for developing lessons and extracurricular activities that are so important to the academic curriculum. In the morning, teachers taught math, Spanish, and science. In the afternoon, they taught history, civics, geography, and "manual arts," such as carpentry, art, and singing. School, she says, was more like home. Students had parties and exhibits where they showed artwork and crafts they had made in their manual arts class. Parents and teachers organized field trips to expand the children's learning into the community. The director recounts that there were fewer learning problems then, since students and families got to know the teachers, and there was time in the day for thorough lessons and related extracurricular programs.

---

48. An interesting contrast, very few principals in the United States have such a sense of the school/neighborhood history, as they are transferred often.

Now, the director laments that field trips are rare; teachers have to write up proposals for excursions and have them approved by an educational coordinator at the state level. Both approval and funding are hard to get. The curriculum, too, has changed; English as a Second Language was not offered until the 1990s, through the program *Construyendo el Futuro*.[49]

TEXAS SCHOOLING/EL PASO SCHOOLING

El Paso has been a major crossroads between east and west in the United States and a gateway connecting Mexico and the United States for a century and a half. El Paso County was formed in 1850, just two years after the signing of the Treaty of Guadalupe. The state authorized public schools in 1854, stipulating that English be taught as a subject (particularly important for those who had been Spanish-speaking Mexican citizens before the treaty). By 1858, the state declared English to be the principal language of instruction, and, later, English became the official medium of instruction.[50]

The city of El Paso was established in 1873, with its first public city schoolroom opening in 1881. In keeping with the tradition of decentralized education in the United States, the county judge appointed a panel of local citizens to investigate the need for public schools. Through popular (male) vote, a school board was elected, with the mayor and county judge serving as ex-officio members.[51]

By 1896, the number of schools in El Paso had grown to three private schools and five public schools, segregating students by racial and

---

49. "Building the Future," a program designed by SEP administrators Gabriela Flores Balbuena, Margarita Gallegos, and Octavio Márquez, in Special Education Programs. The original three foci were ESL, computers, and study habits.

50. Guadalupe San Miguel, *Let Them All Take Heed: Mexican Americans and the Campaign for Educational Equity in Texas, 1910–1981* (Austin: University of Texas Press, 1987).

51. Retired Judge Armendáriz donated boxes of papers associated with the Alvarado case (see pg 40) to the Special Collections Section of the Library at the University of Texas at El Paso. This section draws from this unpublished material unless otherwise noted.

national origin. Douglas Colored Public School and the Mexican Preparatory School offered elementary level education. The 1897–1898 census listed 1,350 students; 116 Mexican American, and eleven "Negro." The Mexican school, later called Aoy School after its founder, was opened as a free private school, and, later, incorporated into one of the larger El Paso school districts.[52]

The Ysleta School District provides an example of the changes in education over the last century. Named after the Ysleta Native American community, it opened its school doors in 1884 in a ranching area that the city of El Paso would later incorporate. Early classes were taught at the old courthouse, rented for educational purposes. In 1916, its roof was used as a lookout to watch for a possible raid by Pancho Villa.[53]

Like many U.S. schools after the 1880–1920 wave of new immigrants, Americanization values permeated the curriculum and school spirit. In 1924, Ysleta's sixth grade class adopted the motto, "I can't is un-American." In the 1930s, Ysleta Elementary boasted that cowboys on horseback practiced roping goats on Sundays on the school playground.

The school had a number of "firsts," including bilingual instruction (against school policy) taught by Mrs. Trixie Spencer for students who had recently arrived from Mexico. Its first woman principal, Miss Vada Gilliland, in 1943–44, stepped in to replace a male principal on active military duty. The original school mascot, the bear, eventually became the Indian (with classroom clusters known as tribes). Ysleta's first Spanish-surname principal, Mr. Rudy Reséndez, served from 1970 to 1979.

While there were exceptions in language policy, teachers in El Paso usually discouraged students from using Spanish. Retired Judge Armendáriz, born in 1919, noted that if students spoke Spanish, they

---

52. Bertha Archer Schaer, "Historical Sketch of Aoy School," El Paso Public Schools, April 27, 1951.

53. "History of Ysleta Elementary School 1884–1989," by class 5–2, unpublished (Ysleta Independent School District).

were treated as "dirty" or "bad." He acknowledged that some teachers were "more eagerly anti-Mexican than others."[54] Insistence on English at schools persisted for a half century. In her autobiography of growing up in El Paso during the 1940s and 1950s, Gloria Stafford-López remembers being caught speaking to her friend in Spanish. The teacher told her, "English is spoken in school . . . even when you are speaking to your friends, young lady! . . . So, Raquel and I had to each stand in a corner of that stupid closet during recess."[55]

The Mexican American educational experience frequently included low expectations from administrators and teachers, and inferior school buildings and materials. In the 1920s and 1930s, property taxes supplied most of the funding, so "property-poor" districts, including El Paso and most places along the border, had less materials, teachers with less professional training, and fewer students graduating from high school. Of the 834 students who graduated from high school in El Paso between 1898 and 1920, only twenty-two were Spanish-surnamed.[56]

El Paso schools, zoned by neighborhoods, segregated those living south of the railroad tracks into "Mexican" schools, and those living north of the tracks into "American" (Anglo) schools, even though almost all residents were U.S. citizens. Segregation was sometimes overridden, however, since housing location was based on income rather than ethnicity. Still, the Mexican-heritage population was over-represented among the poor in south and southeast El Paso near the international border.

This racial profiling in education was met with resistance on sev-

54. Oral History Institute, University of Texas at El Paso, Albert Armendáriz Sr., July 10, 1976, interviewer, Oscar Martínez (#284).

55. Gloria Stafford-López, *A Place in El Paso* (Albuquerque: University of New Mexico Press, 1996), 46–47.

56. Mario Garcia, *Desert Immigrants* (New Haven, Conn.: Yale University Press, 1981), 125; On inequitable funding, see Gregory Rocha and Robert Webking. *Politics and Public Education: Edgewood v. Kirby and the Reform of Public School Financing in Texas,* 2nd ed. (Minneapolis: West Publishing, 1993).

eral fronts—through community organization, the U.S. government, and the courts. In the 1930s and 1940s, a call for equal educational opportunity emerged. Cultural and civil rights organizations, such as the League of United Latin American Citizens (LULAC), struggled against discrimination.[57]

The civil rights movement and federal government response focused their earliest attention on racial segregation in schools in the United States. In 1955, after the *Brown v. Board of Education* ruling, El Paso desegregated its "colored" school. Yet, consistent federal attention to Mexican American students did not emerge until the late 1960s when the Department of Health, Education and Welfare (HEW) gathered an enormous amount of data on five southwestern states, from Texas to California.

Following this, the U.S. Commission on Civil Rights published a six-volume study on ethnic isolation in the schools, entitled the *Mexican American Education Study*. Parts of this study illustrate the deep and pervasive segregation and inequality that permeated public education, especially in the state of Texas. The commission cited a study of 122 school districts in Texas, half of which segregated Mexican American students through the sixth grade. "Language handicap" was the policy rationale.

The most compelling evidence, however, came from the commission's analysis of 1968–69 data from school districts with over 3,000 students throughout the southwest.[58] They found that of those students who stayed in school through twelfth grade, 80 percent were Anglos, 65 percent were black, and 53 percent were Mexican Americans. In English reading, they found that 74 percent of Mexican American students read below grade level compared to 28 percent of Anglos. Looking at students two or more years older than the average age of their classmates in eighth grade (an indicator of potential dropouts),

---

57. See the history of LULAC in Benjamin Márquez. *LULAC: The Evolution of a Mexican American Political Organization* (Austin: University of Texas Press, 1993).

58. *The Mexican American Education Study*, published between 1971 and 1974 (Washington D.C.: U.S. Commission on Civil Rights [CCR]).

they found that in the overage group, 17 percent were Mexican American, and only 2 percent were Anglo.

For all three categories, Texas had the worst profile for educating Mexican Americans in all of the southwest states. Texas also had the highest percent of (monolingual) Spanish-speaking first graders (62 percent) compared to the other southwestern states. In the late 1960s, when bilingual education was just beginning, 6 percent of the Texas schools offered bilingual classes, enrolling only one-half a percent of Mexican American students statewide.[59]

The U.S. Commission on Civil Rights cited two large El Paso school districts as being "non-compliant" with the Civil Rights Act. Both districts, it said, failed to provide educational experiences for Mexican American students as effective as those for Anglo students. The two districts were also cited for their lack of Mexican American teachers and for the discriminatory assignment of Mexican American students to classes for the "emotionally and mentally retarded." In 1972, El Paso entered an agreement with HEW to remedy this non-compliance. Little action occurred, however, until the federal circuit court ordered remedies four years later in 1976.

In the late 1960s time period, few Mexican Americans in Texas worked as teachers, administrators, or school board members. The Commission on Civil Rights reported just 3 percent of Texas school principals were Mexican American, and, among teachers, just 5 percent were Mexican American. El Paso's percentages were higher at this time; almost a third of the teachers and administrators were Mexican American. Anglos won most elected positions—only 5 percent of the state legislators and 7 percent of the school board members were Mexican American.

Building on these reports and a growing Mexican American voice, advocates of a more equitable education for El Paso's children pursued legal strategies. The Mexican American Legal and Defense Education Fund (MALDEF) positioned itself, like the National Association for the Advancement of Colored People (NAACP), to pursue systemic change in policy and public finance through the courts.

---

59. Volume 3 of the CCR report focuses on language.

A national system of decentralized education allowed separate and discriminatory practices to exist, but a national discourse of social justice was used to dismantle these practices. In 1970, fourteen parents initiated a class action suit, *Alvarado, et al. v. El Paso Independent School District*, against El Paso's largest school district for operating and maintaining a "dual and racially segregated school system in violation of the Fourteenth Amendment to the United States Constitution."[60] Massive amounts of data were analyzed for patterns of segregation among students and teacher assignments, for neighborhood school zoning with intent to segregate, and for inferior education to Mexican American students. Ruling on the case in 1976, the judge found deliberate "segregative intent" in school boundaries and teacher placement.

The judge's remedies included busing, redrawing school boundaries, increased recruitment of Mexican American administrators and faculty, and bilingual-bicultural educational programs. The *Alvarado* case marked a turning point for El Paso education, reinforced with increased federal support for bilingual education in high-poverty neighborhoods.

Structural racism, however, persisted for Mexican Americans, in spite of desegregation. Counselors encouraged students to go into vocational tracks, which did not prepare them for higher education and the opportunity for upward mobility. Rules against speaking Spanish in school persisted through the 1960s. The Mexican American Youth Association (MAYA) was founded in 1969 to fight the suppression of the Spanish language. One of the students in this association described being punished for speaking Spanish:

> Being detained after school for an hour . . . being hit with a ruler in
> the hand, or being swatted or being forced to make push-ups, like I

---

60. Thanks to historian Kenton Clymer for copies of the Findings, Defendants, and Memorandum Opinion and Order from *Alvarado v. EPISD*, decided 1976, and to the Armendáriz papers in Special Collections, UTEP Library. Isela Peña located all the clippings from the *El Paso Times*, circa early 1976, on this historic case. El Paso County has nine school districts and nine sets of school board trustees, keeping with the U.S. decentralization structure.

was, in front of the class. It wasn't only me; everybody got the same treatment. Sometimes, if it got real bad, you had to bring your parents to talk to the assistant principal and explain why you were acting with such bad conduct.[61]

MAYA's activism resulted in replacing two anti-Spanish assistant principals with Mexican Americans.[62]

More recently, reform movements have transferred local control of education to the state level through legislation and accountability testing. Texas responded to the 1983 national report *A Nation at Risk* by strengthening teacher certification requirements, imposing a testing system on teachers and students, and reducing elementary class sizes to twenty-two students.[63] The report, using alarmist, nationalist language to warn against mediocrity, claimed, "If an unfriendly foreign power had attempted to impose on America the mediocre educational performance that exists today, we might well have viewed it as an act of war."[64]

Previous decentralized control over education had allowed for persistent neglect of Mexican American students. National intervention made this neglect visible, providing leverage for local civil rights and educational advocates to press for equal educational opportunity in the courts.

---

61. Oral History Institute, UTEP, Fred Morales, interviewed by Oscar Martínez, March 16, 1976 (#211), 3–4; Javier Salgado, "Awakenings in the Segundo Barrio: Mexican American Youth Association (MAYA) 1967–1972," M.A. Seminar Paper, University of Texas at El Paso, 1998.

62. Volume 3, U.S. Commission on Civil Rights.

63. On the last two decades of Texas reform, see Dennis Shirley, *Community Organizing for Urban School Reform* (Austin: University of Texas Press, 1997), chap. 2; LBJ School of Public Affairs, *Preparing for the Twenty-first Century: Public Education Reform in Texas* (Austin: Policy Research Project #107).

64. U.S. National Commission on Excellence in Education, "A Nation at Risk: The Imperative for Educational Reform" (Washington, D.C.: National Commission on Excellence in Education, 1983).

EL PASO AND JUÁREZ CONTRASTS

National policies, bureaucracies, and organized teachers' interests shape both cities in the border metroplex. Contrasts in the two cities exist in many areas of education: grade level divisions, funding sources, school governance, school names, attendance and truancy policies, teacher salaries, and teacher unions.

Table 1 contrasts some of the El Paso and Juárez differences. Grade divisions are fairly similar: elementary, secondary, and high school, completed in twelve years, although the *preparatoria* years in Mexico are spent specifically preparing for higher education. The length of the school year is also roughly equivalent, with El Paso requiring 180 days and Juárez 200. In El Paso, the school day is slightly longer—six to seven hours, compared to five hours in Juárez. Most public elementary schools in Juárez have two shifts, morning and afternoon.

Funding and governance in both cities are totally different. It took a lawsuit and a series of legislative reforms to help create a more equitable funding system in Texas with current per pupil spending at approximately $5,000 annually. Until funding became more equitable in the mid-1990s, borderland students and the Mexican Americans who make up the vast majority scored far below students in other parts of the state on the Texas Academic Achievement System (TAAS) tests.[65]

In the state of Texas there are approximately 1,000 independent school districts. El Paso County's nine school districts are each governed by an elected seven-member school board. The two largest districts, educating 62,000 and 45,000 students, respectively, are classified among the ten largest districts in the state. Juárez, by contrast, enrolls

---

65. John Sharp, *Bordering the Future: Challenge and Opportunity in the Texas Border Regions* (Austin: Texas Comptroller of Public Accounts, 1998), chap. 3. Figures on per pupil spending in Texas come from the Texas Education Agency website, Academic Indicator Excellence System, reported out by state and school district. See also Rocha and Webking, 1993.

TABLE 1. EDUCATION CONTRASTS: EL PASO, TX/U.S.–JUÁREZ, CHIH/MEXICO

EL PASO	JUÁREZ
Grade Divisions	
Elementary 1–5 or 6	*Primaria* 1–6
Middle 6 or 7–8	*Secundaria* 1–3 (grades 7, 8, 9)
High 9–12	*Preparatoria* 1–3 (grades 10, 11, 12)
Governance	
Federal	
Dept. of Education	Secretaría de Educación Pública
State	
Texas Education Agency	State SEP office
Elected State Board of Education	Nothing comparable
Local	
Elected School Boards	Nothing comparable
Independent School Districts	Nothing comparable
Governance Trends	
Centralization (at state level)	Decentralization
Expenditures per Pupil	
approx. $5,000	less than 8,000 pesos ($800 US)
Revenue	
State, then local (property)	Federal, then state
Textbooks	
Commercial	SEP (free at *primaria* level)
Calendar/Days	
180 days per year	200 days per year
6–7 hours daily	5 hours daily
one shift	generally two shifts

150,000 students as part of the Zona Norte[66] of the SEP state office in Chihuahua City, the state capital.

Mexico has nothing equivalent to U.S. school boards, public interest lawsuits, or educational lobby groups, factors which make centralized decisionmaking in Mexico all the more significant. Mexico has increased its educational spending to 6 percent of its national budget from the period of the revolution to a 1930s high point in funding to current times. Nearly half of the budget is spent on elementary education where the largest number of students is concentrated. Although Mexico does not report expenditures the same way as the United States, we estimate that elementary education spending in Chihuahua is less than $800 per pupil annually.[67]

Teachers' starting annual salaries in El Paso when we began this study in 1994 ranged from $21,000 to $24,000 for a nine-month period. By the year 2000, starting salaries approached $30,000. At the elementary levels, the vast majority of teachers are women working in a feminized profession with comparatively low salaries. Many join professional teaching associations in Texas, but by law they are prohibited from collective bargaining or striking.

All Mexican teachers belong to the largest union in Latin America, the Sindicato Nacional de Trabajadores de la Educación[68] (SNTE), with membership surpassing a million, most of whom are women. Although factions have occasionally demonstrated a critical

---

66. Northern Zone.

67. "Educational Investment," SEP's website (www.sep.gob.mx) reports a 7,000 peso average expenditure per student for 1999, equivalent to $700 annually for a population aged three to twenty-five enrolled in public schools (expanding beyond *preparatoria*). Enrique Cabrero Mendoza in chap. 6, "Education," in *New Federalism and State Government in Mexico*, ed. Peter Ward and Victoria Rodríguez, points out that the federal government contributes 50 to 70 percent of the funds. The state SEP administrators we talked to put a state price tag per pupil at the equivalent of $50. Educational expert on Latin America, Nellie Stromquist, reported the equivalent of $100 annually for countries in the region in 1989 (a time when U.S. educational spending per pupil averaged $3,700. Nellie Stromquist, *Women in Education in Latin America* (Boulder, Colo.: Lynne Rienner, 1992), 21–22.

68. National Union of Education Workers.

militancy, its leadership usually collaborates closely with the national government. Union leadership is networked with political decision makers in "symbiotic" ways:

> The government lets the union act—vertically, corporatively, and corruptly—as well as designate educational officials, supervisors, and even school principals. Union committees decide on positions and movements of teachers all over the nation. The power this gives the union can be easily imagined. In exchange, the federal government expects political tranquility on the side of the teachers.[69]

While Mexican teachers may seem powerful as a group, their wages tell a different story. According to the Foundation for Teachers' Culture, a majority of teachers hold two teaching jobs to make ends meet. Primary teachers earn an average of the U.S. equivalent of $300 to $800[70] monthly, depending on seniority and education.

Parents also have an influence on education, though usually in minor ways. In the United States, Parent-Teacher Associations and Organizations (PTAs and PTOs) have huge memberships, although their roles in schools range from minimal fund-raising to more rarely shared policymaking; they have declined markedly since their peak in the 1960s. Neither El Paso nor Juárez has a long tradition of sustained civic activism in education, especially for low-income parents, although parents are encouraged to volunteer in schools and monitor homework.

In a study of Mexican educational reform, parents have been called "the outcasts of the educational process."[71] But parents connect with

---

69. Reyes Heroles, quoted in Sylvia Schmelkes, "The Problems of the Decentralization of Education: A View from Mexico," in *Latin American Education: Comparative Perspectives,* ed. Carlos Alberto Torres and Adriana Puiggros (Boulder: Westview, 1977), 150.

70. Kathleen Staudt, *Policy, Politics, and Gender: Women Gaining Ground* (West Hartford, Conn.: Kumarian Press, 1998), chap. 4.

71. Guillermo Trejo, "The Politics of Educational Reform in Mexico: Ambivalence toward Change," in *The Challenge of Institutional Reform in Mexico.* ed. Riordan Roett (Boulder, Colo.: Lynne Rienner, 1995), 134.

schools in national and cultural school calendar celebrations like *día de las Madres*, for example, in making considerable contributions for materials and fees, on rare occasions in participating in school-organized councils, and in volunteerism. For many, there is a profound respect for teachers and schools. Rarely, though, do parents critique or challenge schools, an orientation that undermines parental engagement when transnational migrants to the United States enroll their children in U.S. schools. Occasionally, newspapers contain headlines about parents who have organized to protest corruption and abuse in schools, but these are usually short term in nature and center around a single issue.

Both the United States and Mexico have compulsory education through secondary school, but in the United States, funding formulas are tied to attendance, so administrators and teachers are often zealous about enforcement. In Mexico, education is obligatory to age fourteen, but lack of schools and truancy officers limit implementation.

Textbook selection is also quite different in both countries. The SEP takes full control of the curriculum and of the textbooks, creating and distributing these free, obligatory books to each student at every school throughout the republic. In the United States, textbook companies are entirely commercial; Texas school districts purchase textbooks after lengthy adoption processes, and then lend them to students for an academic year. Texas and California, because of their large populations, often lead in the adoption of textbooks and other states follow their example.

School names reveal a community's celebration of identity and what it claims as its heritage. El Paso tends to choose names related more to local history, whereas Juárez school names are often related to national history. Browsing the Texas Education Agency website,[72] we found thirty-three schools named after Jim Bowie of Alamo renown, compared with twenty-two for Thomas Jefferson and sixteen for George Washington. By this indicator, Texas heroes are valued more than national heroes.

---

72. www.tea.state.tx.us

We compared use of local and regional names and inauguration dates in elementary, middle, and high schools in a large El Paso school district with those present elsewhere in the United States (Table 2).

The first bar compares Texan and United States heroes in naming schools, showing that more Texan than U.S. heroes and heroic places are used to name schools. The second bar compares surnames of local characters, showing that Anglo surnames, mostly male, outnumber Spanish surnames by three to one. The third bar compares local places that have Spanish and English names, showing a balance of neighborhoods using both languages. The dates when the schools opened show that Spanish surnames are given more often in the 1990s period. We find no international or global names used in this region.

We considered doing a similar school name bar graph for Juárez, but almost all names are national in focus: military figures, presidents, dates of historical events, births and deaths of prominent leaders. A sampling of school names include Vicente Guerrero (military leader), 20 de Noviembre (the Mexican Revolution), Mi Patria es Primero (my country is first), Cinco de Mayo (date the French were expelled from Mexico), Revolución (for the Mexican Revolution of 1910), Ignacio Zaragoza (military leader), Francisco Villa (revolutionary leader based in northern Mexico), 21 de Marzo (birth of Benito Juárez, past president), Lázaro Cardenas (reformist president), and 18 de Julio (death of Benito Juárez). The Juárez school names also include international personalities, including intellectuals and inventors Jean Piaget and Leonardo da Vinci, adventurer Cristóbal Colon (known as Christopher Columbus in the United States), Aztec leader Cuauhtémoc, former Chilean president Salvador Allende, and several international writers. A handful of names offer special appeal to children, such as Blanca Nieves.[73] Internationalism and global perspectives are important to Mexico's historical place in the world.[74]

---

73. Snow White.

74. See www.sep.gob.mx, the SEP's home page.

TABLE 2. EL PASO INDEPENDENT SCHOOL DISTRICT: CAMPUS NAMES

Heroes/Heroic Places

Texas		*United States*	
Bowie (1973)	Roberts (1951)	Chapin (2000)	Wainwright (1949)
Fannin (1963)	Burleson (1951)	Lee (1982)	Roosevelt (1947)
Lamar (1962)	Travis (1950)	Lindbergh (1981)	Hawkins (1942)
Ross (1960)	Austin (1930)	Bradley (1981)	Douglass (1920)
Logan (1960)	Zavala (1927)	Johnson (1974)	
Henderson (1958)	Houston (1922)	Lincoln (1971)	
Burnet (1955)	Crockett (1920)	MacArthur (1965)	
Bonham (1954)	Rusk (1915)	Bliss (1958)	
Milam (1953)	Alamo (1899)	Jefferson (1949)	

Local Heroes (Surnames)

English		*Spanish*
Nolan Richardson (1998)	Irvin (1959)	Paul Moreno (1999)
Olga Kohlberg (1997)	Stanton (1959)	Cordova (1999)
Dr. Green (1993)	Putnam (1959)	Silva Magnet (1994)
Whitaker (1987)	Dowell (1959)	Dr. Hornedo (1994)
Wiggs (1987)	Crosby (1958)	Guerrero (1992)
Clendenin (1983)	Bassett (1957)	Rivera (1975)
Polk (1981)	Hart (1957)	Guillen (1973)
Dr. Nixon (1981)	Magoffin (1956)	Coronado (1962)
Collins (1979)	Burges (1955)	Aoy (1899)
Charles (1975)	Clardy (1954)	
White (1968)	Hughey (1953)	
Morehead (1965)	Cooley (1952)	
Schuster (1963)	Coldwell (1930)	
Andress (1961)	Vilas (1909)	
Park (1961)	Beall (1907)	
Newman (1960)		

Local Places (References)

English		*Spanish*	
Franklin (1993)	Western Hills (1963)	Cielo Vista (1968)	Alta Vista (1912)
Terrace Hills (1962)	Hillside (1950)	Mesita (1948)	
Canyon Hills (1973)		El Paso (1916)	

CONCLUSION

The area we now know as El Paso and Juárez has a rich multicultural history; Native American, Spanish colony, the Mexican Republic, the Republic of Texas, and finally Texas statehood. Since its origins as a northern Mexican frontier town to its separation into two cities and two nations, children have experienced unique educational differences and nationalist agendas. Educational organization and school names are symbols of this historical legacy.

With the Treaty of Guadalupe Hidalgo, Mexicans became conquered adversaries and new community members in their own land. Schools set up for English-speaking Anglo Americans rarely took the education of Mexican Americans seriously. The result was a two-tiered educational system that included inferior school buildings and materials, and lower teacher expectations for the "new" Americans. Decentralized control over education in the United States allowed for persistent neglect of Mexican American students. Federal intervention made this neglect visible, providing leverage for local civil rights and educational advocates to press for equal educational opportunity in the courts.

Today bilingualism is the norm in El Paso public schools, and English classes are being initiated in Juárez public schools. Mexican American children in El Paso are neglected less as more Mexican Americans have become teachers, and as teachers become more sensitive to diversity. Additionally, state and national accountability checks encourage teachers and administrators to make sure that all students in their schools are learning (or at least passing standardized tests).

In both countries, education has gone through tremendous transformation. The two cities, El Paso and Juárez have grown individually, but they remain interdependent and continue to influence each other, espousing a more practical, social experience for children. While the SEP and U.S. standards impose conformity, they also attempt to provide bases for equity.

CHAPTER 3

Nationalism, Civics, and Education

La patria es nuestra tierra, la tierra de nuestros padres. La queremos como se quiere a la familia, al lugar done vivimos, al paisaje que nos rodea. No la amamos porque sea grande y poderosa, ni por débil y pequeña. La amamos, simplemente, porque es la nuestra. La patria está representada, está como guardada, en los Símbolos Patrios, que son el Escudo, La Bandera y el Himno Nacionales.[75]

Through texts such as the one above, children in Juárez are taught to love and accept their nation like they love and accept their family, simply because it is theirs. These early lessons on patriotism enlarge on a sense of loyalty to family and to a love of nation as a larger sense of personal identity. Reminders of nationalist symbols and national identities are part of everyday life, but does reading about national symbols and promising loyalty to them inspire patriotism? And does it lead to informed civic engagement?

---

75. The country, is our land, the land of our parents. We love it like we love family, the place where we live, the landscape that surrounds us. We don't love it because it is big and powerful, or because it is weak and small. We love it simply because it is ours. The country is represented and guarded by the National Symbols, which are the national Coat of Arms, Flag and Anthem. Fourth grade history book. In *Historia Cuarto Grado* (México, D.F.: Secretaría de Educación Pública, 1996), 176.

Photo by Susan Rippberger

Courtyard flag salute, Juárez School.

HONORES A LA BANDERA — JUÁREZ

Benito Juárez School children crowd in through the front gate on Monday morning, some accompanied by their parents, others with siblings and neighborhood friends. As they arrive in the central courtyard, they find their teacher who shepherds them into line with their classmates. Everyone at the school—the custodian, volunteer parents, and support staff—assembles for the ceremony. The director greets students warmly, *"Buenos días, alumnos,"* as children are hushed by their teachers and encouraged to get in straight lines and stand at attention.

A third grade boy, guided by the director, leads the school in reciting the pledge. He commands formally, *"Saludar ya,"*[76] as flag bearers, dressed in full military uniform, march in, goose stepping, clicking their heels as they make sharp right angle turns. For this ceremony, a sixth grade girl bears the flag. She is flanked by color guards and a

---

76. Ready, Salute.

drum and trumpet core, also in full uniform. Students, teachers, and others stand at attention with their right arm held precisely at a right angle to their chest, hand flat, parallel to their heart. *"Bandera de México legado de nuestros heroes, símbolo de la unidad de nuestros padres y de nuestros hermanos. Te prometemos (*at this point, the pledgers thrust their arm straight forward toward the flag, hand flat, thumb slightly under their forefinger*) ser siempre fieles a los principios de libertad y de justicia que hacen de nuestro patria la nación independiente, humana y generosa, a la que entregamos nuestra existencia."*[77] The third grader then commands, *"Firmes ya,"*[78] and students put their arms down and remain at attention for the national anthem. The director, accompanied by a record player, leads the school in singing the national anthem that begins, *"Mexicanos, al grito de guerra."*[79]

Following the national anthem, the flag bearer and color guard march out to drums and trumpets and the director makes announcements for the day, encouraging each child to study hard and excel in their studies. Students then file out by class, starting with the youngest, led by their teachers to their classrooms where instruction begins.

THE FLAG SALUTE—EL PASO

Children enter their second grade bilingual classroom at Schuster School, sitting at their assigned desks. The teacher greets them, and takes roll. Each day about this time, the principal's voice comes over the loudspeaker near the ceiling, "Good morning students. Please stand for the flag salute." The teacher, her assistant, and the students stand at their desks and face the flag mounted on the wall. They drape their right hand over their chest, and recite the pledge with the overhead voice, "I pledge

---

77. Flag of Mexico, legacy of our heroes, symbol of the unity of our parents and our brothers [and sisters]. We promise to be always faithful to the principles of liberty and justice, that make our nation independent, humane, and generous, and to which we offer our very existence.

78. At attention.

79. Mexicans, at the cry of war . . .

Photo by Susan Rippberger

Five year olds, presenting, Honores a la Bandera.

allegiance to the flag of the United States of America, and to the republic for which it stands. One nation under God, indivisible, with liberty
and justice for all." Students stand casually, politely, some repeating dis-
tinctly all the words, others mouthing the words to the best of their ability, some stumbling over difficult parts. Afterward, they remain standing
to sing the national anthem: "Oh, say can you see!" they begin enthusiastically. After the singing, the principal announces special events for the
day, and encourages students to do their best. The U.S. national anthem,
like Mexico's, is one of war, triumph, and fervent patriotism. But what
do adults think students are learning directly or indirectly—love of country, unquestioned tradition, or just another ritual?

The flag ceremony in Mexico is repeated every Monday, in public
and private schools all over Mexico. Students assemble in the central
courtyard to pay honor to their flag and to their nation. Schools compete citywide in the performance of this formal, stylized ritual. They
are judged according to precision, neatness, and ability, receiving training from preschool on up. The expectation is that students are learning
nationalism as well as formality, respect, tradition, and obedience.

In Juárez, a third grader always leads the pledge, because that is the year they first formally study the meaning of the flag salute and national anthem. On February 24, *el Día de la Bandera*,[80] all third graders from public and private schools attend a citywide flag ceremony, *al Juarmento de la Bandera*,[81] at the local university. Here they discuss the importance of the flag, what the colors mean (green: hope, white: peace, and red: the blood spilled during the independence movement), and they learn how to carry the flag and execute the flag ceremony.

In many classrooms across the United States, students rise to recite the pledge of allegiance, and some schools include the national anthem. Some line up under the flag, others remain at their desks. Some schools begin schoolwide assemblies with the flag salute; others do not. In contrast to Mexican flag rituals, the U.S. flag salute is becoming more of an individual exercise, a choice made by each student, a chance to reflect on the meaning of the pledge; for example, is this really a country where liberty and justice is for all, or are some more privileged because of gender, skin color, or class?[82]

The flag salute in either country, as proxy for civic learning, offers insights into children's early training in nationalism. Pledging national allegiance is commonplace in schools, where children are taught to affirm their national loyalty, but how deeply this is internalized is not clear. Teachers do try to teach meaning beyond mere memorization of the words, through classroom discussion, and in Mexico specifically by making the topic a memorable social experience for children in the third grade.

We asked El Paso and Juárez teachers to react to the videos of the two nation's flag ceremonies. They noted first the contrast in formality. A third grade El Paso teacher observed the casualness of the U.S. flag salute: "The flag ceremony is just a ritual we go through every day." A

---

80. Flag Day.

81. Swearing allegiance to the flag.

82. See Mark Singer, "I Pledge Allegiance: A Liberal Town's School System Meets the New Patriotism," *New Yorker*, November 26, 2001, 54–61.

Mexican administrator directing Special Programs for the state noted that *Honores a la Bandera* went beyond the important civic lessons found in the pledge itself to other related social values, explaining with an authoritarian slant,

> It teaches order, organization, precision, community. It is a ceremony, a ritual that is to be respected without question. The U.S. flag ceremony, on the other hand, is very short, unorganized, individualistic, and overall, unimpressive.

Teachers in El Paso and Juárez both acknowledge the advanced vocabulary and complex concepts in their respective flag salutes. Not only bilingual students but also English speakers have great difficulty with the words. Many children (even English speakers) say "invisible" rather than "indivisible." A sixth grade Mexican American student, when asked to write out the pledge, wrote the last phrase: "with liverty [sic] and just a frog." We wondered how much nationalism is instilled or resisted with this type of creative interpretation.

An El Paso teacher told us, "I put the words to the pledge and anthem on the wall so the kids can follow along. But I always have to teach the meaning—'Ramparts,' for example, is very hard for them." A student teacher at Vilas School displayed students' colorful pictures on hallway walls with illustrated phrases from the pledge. She said she decided to engage students in this exercise after she heard students saying "invisible" instead of "indivisible." Teachers often decorate classroom walls with posters that have the words to the pledge.

Mexican teachers had similar experiences in trying to teach the larger concepts found in their flag salute. One explained, "*Honores a la bandera* is fine, but the students need to learn what it all means, including the patriotism—not just the marching and saluting, but why you salute and what the flag means."

Looking for other perspectives on the flag ceremony, we showed the video to a group of students raised in Juárez, but taking introductory classes taught in Spanish at the university in El Paso. One student said the Mexican flag ritual was holistic, with the whole school present, the ceremony, and the color guards all representing patriotism on different levels. When they heard the *Himno Nacional* on the video, they spontaneously sang along. A love of country, or perhaps the feeling of community and pride it brought out in these students, was apparent. U.S. students viewing the same video commented on the overly militaristic character of the ritual.

Civic education attempts to prepare students for social responsibility and participation, giving them knowledge about and commitment to community, political institutions, and public affairs. In both countries civic education goes further, constructing and supporting national myths of unity, sovereignty, and abstract principles of patriotism and loyalty.

NATIONAL HOLIDAYS

National holidays provide teachers in Juárez and El Paso with opportunities for teaching nationalist themes and values. Many plan activities and projects around holidays. During a visit to observe ESL lessons in Juárez, the day before a national holiday, we observed a group of fifteen to twenty teachers preparing for the celebration of the 20th of November, *día de la revolución*.[83] The teachers had an old phonograph playing traditional music on the playground and were practicing folk dances, while uniformed groups of first and second grade girls gathered around to watch and imitate the teachers' dance steps. In preparation for the celebration, teachers in public and private schools ready their students for a city parade, parent presentations, meals, and dances.

Teachers in El Paso also plan activities and lessons around national holidays, although students often take vacations on the holiday itself so there are fewer citywide school-related events. Thanksgiving and Presidents' Day in U.S. elementary schools, for example, are the basis for vocabulary lessons, art activities, and social studies projects. Before Thanksgiving, first grade children learn about Squanto, in romanti-

---

83. Day of the Revolution (1910).

cized stories that illustrate cooperation between Native Americans and British immigrants. More open portrayals of Native Americans in middle school textbooks later discuss the Trail of Tears, the broken treaties, and the near genocide. In Mexico, too, romanticized versions of indigenous populations are collapsed into one noble Aztec "race," whereas modern-day Native Mexicans continue to be economically and socially marginalized.

In U.S. elementary schools, Presidents' Day in February, efficiently commemorating Washington's and Lincoln's birthdays together, is celebrated with idealized stories about the presidents' childhoods. Students cut out silhouettes of the presidents' heads in art classes, and teachers read to them stories of cherry trees and about not telling lies.

VOTING AND CIVIC ACTIVITY IN SCHOOLS

Children are exposed to their place in civil society in many ways, from patriotic background music like "Texas Our Texas" in El Paso classrooms to discussions on *día de los muertos*[84] and Halloween in Juárez schools. Children pledge national allegiance, hear about values and character, and learn specific details about their local and national histories. They learn how to vote, but usually on trivial issues. For example, in El Paso classrooms, voting for chalk monitor or even classroom president, that is, the teacher's helper, can create an illusion of democracy in a system where agendas are already set by teachers, administration, or state legislatures. Children do not vote on issues that affect them, such as the time school should start, or whether or not to take standardized testing. Neither do parents nor teachers for that matter.

In a Juárez first grade social studies lesson, students learned about voting as they planned their Christmas party. The teacher listed their favorite party foods on the chalkboard: pizza, hamburgers, hot dogs, and nachos (ironically, typical U.S. food). Students were asked to vote for the one food they wanted to have at the party. Not quite under-

---

84. Day of the Dead, a commemoration on November 2 of those who have gone before us.

State nationalism, El Paso school hallway.

Photo by Kathleen Staudt

standing the process, they raised their hands for each of the menu items they liked. In the end, teachers and room mothers decided on one of the choices based on cost and ease of preparation.

Children learn civic activity and practice the process of democracy in ways that are more meaningful than voting for class monitor or party food. Children in the United States can take part in national elections, and in Mexico, children vote for civic ideals. Kids Voting/USA and Mexico's La Elección es tambien Nuestros[85] are national initiatives for children to learn more about national elections. Both are nonpartisan efforts to promote voting, voting skills, and knowledge about public decisions. They differ in that in Mexico children vote for their rights, not for candidates; and in the United States, kids vote for individual

---

85. The Election is Ours too.

candidates, not parties or issues. Mexican children vote for rights that come from a list of rights developed through the United Nations Children Fund (UNICEF), such as the right to an education or to a safe environment.

Mexico's national elections are held during the summer, after school is out, so there is little connection of this experience with teachers and students. The media, however, give the elections extensive visibility, as they do for other experiential activities such as (child) *Presidente Municipal*[86] for the day, visits to the governor, and so on. All over the country, the Instituto Federal Electoral[87] (IFE) manages the effort, as does the local IFE office in Juárez. IFE produces eye-catching and colorful material, in comic book and poster forms, about rights and voting. In 1997, IFE set up 9,000 polling stations for children throughout Mexico. Children voted for rights they felt were most important: the right to education and the right for children to avoid mistreatment got the most votes.

Kids Voting/El Paso is a civic organization that raises funds and recruits volunteers to staff precincts on election day.[88] It is affiliated with Kids Voting/USA, a large national nonprofit organization. While kids' votes are not counted for victory or loss, their participation is an educational process that also expands the political agenda through making candidates more aware of children and family issues. In the 1996 presidential elections, many teachers attended newspaper-sponsored workshops and received materials on ways to weave voting into reading, math, art, and social studies lessons. As a result, 40,000 El Paso children turned out to vote. In 2000, the next presidential election, this figure jumped to 50,000 with no subsidy from the government, but with long hours of volunteerism and university students' service learning.

---

86. Mayor.

87. Federal Electoral Institute, and Lorena Orozco "Civic Education in the State of Morelos" (master's thesis, University of Texas at El Paso, 1998).

88. Kathleen Staudt participated in Kids Voting/El Paso, and she has served on the board since 1996.

Kids Voting, El Paso.

Kids Voting campaign, El Paso teacher.

CAMPUS CEREMONIES

Students are continually given messages that show what we value as civic behavior. Civics is taught in explicit ways through civics lessons, flag salutes, extracurricular activities, such as kids' voting, and indirectly in what is referred to as the hidden curriculum. The way a teacher organizes her classroom can indicate what she and administrators value and wish to promote as civic or "proper." School ceremonies, too, not only celebrate civic behavior but also encourage what is valued. Citizenship awards for good grades or perfect attendance are examples.

El Paso elementary schools hold periodic award ceremonies to affirm certain behavior in children. One such ceremony, to honor achievement and character, took place at Vilas School's auditorium. The flag is placed prominently on the stage, and a mural of the border, with two eagles, one representing the United States, the other representing Mexico, forms a backdrop. One of the most important awards was for good grades, called the "A" Honor Roll and the "A-B" Honor Roll, with certificates for all who earn A and B grades. To encourage students for their efforts, a "BUG" award for "Bringing Up Grades" was given to students who had not attained all As and Bs but had improved. Perfect attendance awards were given out, too. Not only does perfect attendance boost funding for public schools but also it allows for more consistent instruction. Thus, being present was a sign of being a good citizen.

Another important award in this and other El Paso schools is for "citizenship." At the Vilas ceremony, the principal engaged students in an interactive conversation: "What is good citizenship?" Enthusiastic students raised their hands, to be called on in order: "listening to the teacher"; "not fighting"; "following the rules"; "helping others." "Citizenship" in this case involves individual civility and classroom control more than nationalism.

By the time the award ceremony was over, most students had received some type of award. In elementary school, individual or group competition is frequently coupled with egalitarianism that affirms the esteem of all. Lessons on civics underlie these ceremonies, promoting school harmony, consistent attendance, individual achievement, and conformity. The connection between civics education and nationalism is less direct here, but the underlying message of achievement and conformity shows what we value.

VALUES AND CHARACTER

Civic education in both cities frequently includes civility: encouraging "nice" behavior. Schools have long been involved in values education, whether explicit or not, from admonitions about cheating along with encouragement to share with others to references on honesty about presidents "who cannot tell a lie." Juárez and El Paso schools also have formal explicit programs on virtue and civility. In the El Paso classrooms, we saw posters on walls supporting values from flossing your teeth to neighborliness. Posters also warned students against smoking cigarettes and using drugs. The D.A.R.E. (Drug Abuse Resistance Education) program, operating nationwide, draws in police and sheriff deputies to cooperate on education against drugs, with an annual red-ribbon day encouraging students to "Just say, 'No'" to drugs. Posters, classroom discussions on responsibility, conflict-mediation training for student peers, and campus-wide anti-drug events make points about values.

We found similar themes in Juárez schools, with Instituto Federal Electoral posters promoting values like dialogue, tolerance, and liberty. On a wall of Benito Juárez School was a student-created poster of an "X"ed out cigarette and the words "Smoking can cause serious illness: don't smoke." This student's work came from a unit taught by a fifth grade teacher, in coordination with a schoolwide antismoking, anti-vice campaign.

Some Juárez schools promote civility with a weekly virtue such as honesty or patience celebrated at the beginning of each week. In one school we visited, students assembled in the courtyard to discuss "sincerity," the virtue for that week. They watched a short puppet show put on by students illustrating this specific virtue showing how important it is to be straight forward, honest, and humble. The school director

IFE poster on tolerance, Juárez School.

then reinforced the virtue, encouraging students to practice it through-out the week. Teachers followed up with discussions of "sincerity" in their classrooms throughout the week.

Formal lessons on civics and values are also found in SEP textbooks. In a second grade unit on the community, children learn about their neighborhood, the people who live in it, its history, the environment, work, and some of the rights and responsibilities of its members. One of the rights and responsibilities is to get along, by getting to know one another, engaging in dialogue, and organizing to resolve community problems. Some of the obligations listed include knowing and exercising one's rights, such as electing public leaders, using public services, and making sure those in authority respect them. Another is the right of chil-dren *and* adults to play. Children play, the book says, because they have energy, imagination, and the need to get to know other children and have fun. Adults play to relax and enjoy the company of friends.[89] Clearly a people-friendly, community-oriented outlook is valued here.

---

89. Secretaría de Educación Pública, *Libro integrado, Segundo Grado* (México, D.F.: Comisión Nacional de los Libros de Texto Gratuitos, 1966), 74–76.

The IFE, in its effort to promote civics and voting, offers enrichment materials that resemble the board game "Chutes and Ladders." The chutes are replaced with snakes, a prominent symbol on the Mexican flag. In the game, students get ahead (move up the ladder) as they cross paths with values like liberty, impartiality, truthfulness, confidence, justice, respect, pluralism, dialogue, participation, consensus, legality, and voting. Players fall behind, slipping down the snake tails to the fangs, by getting close to intolerance, nonparticipation, dogmatism, abstentionism (nonvoting), conflict, injustice, and partiality. The winner ends by crossing the goal line into *conducto democrática*.[90]

In El Paso, several schools and one whole district have purchased a similar Character Education Program, complete with posters and crafts that stress values such as responsibility, respect, integrity, caring, honesty, cooperation, and perseverance. The Texas State Commission of Education recommended a program called Building Good Citizens for Texas, Resource Guide, in 1996 listing honesty, responsibility, compassion, perseverance, loyalty, justice, self-reliance, self-discipline, and integrity, as values for good citizens. The Institute for American Values helped develop the guide, but it added a special Texas character, including values such as courage, faith, determination, independence, and multiculturalism. The Texas program is as much about individualism and civility as it is about civics and citizenship.

Juárez schools also use a values program that is similar to the "Good Citizens for Texas" values program. Grupo Progreso, an independent community group whose members come from wealthy families, has developed Programa Valores.[91] Their curricular materials, developed with the expertise of educators and published in 1998, include workbooks, teacher handbooks, and materials. With this program, parents are given specific training so they can discuss the values with their children at home. Values they promote include friendship, patriotism, solidarity, environmentalism, respect, courage, perseverance, order, responsibility, diligence, generosity, temperance, all

---

90. Democratic conduct.

91. Values Program.

grouped under the general categories of justice, fortitude, self-control, and prudence.

U.S. and Mexican curricula share many common values, such as courage, perseverance, and responsibility. Collective values, such as solidarity, patriotism, friendship, and generosity appear stronger in Mexico, as do authority themes of respect and order. The U.S. list seems to focus more on an individual point of reference, stressing such values as self-reliance, self-discipline, and independence, although it does include multiculturalism as a value. On the theme of patriotism, a Phi Delta Kappa survey of educators, published in 1995,[92] confirms that people in the United States do not agree on whether Americans respect the U.S. flag enough. Many of the values on the Mexican and U.S. lists are noble, offering mixes of individualism and community, justice and self-direction.

In Juárez, the concept of patriotism is taught as the ability to act with love for the nation, giving tribute to the honor due it, strengthening and defending the blend of values it represents. Students are expected to relate to concepts like *"Es un orgullo ser Mexicano,"*[93] *"Como Mexico no hay dos,"*[94] *"Lo hecho en Mexico está bien hecho,"*[95] and *"Querer la patria es querer la vida."*[96] These affirmations of solidarity build pride, but they do not invite much critical analysis.

Patriotism, in the students' workbook, falls under the general category of justice. In the second grade workbook, illustrations help students distinguish Mexican traditions from non-Mexican traditions, such as the Day of the Dead and Halloween, the latter identified as a "countervalue." In a third grade workbook, students are asked to pick which picture is more Mexican: the flag or the golden arches (of McDonald's).

---

92 . Phi Delta Kappa (PDK), *Values on Which We Agree* (Bloomington, Ind.: Phi Delta Kappa, 1996).

93. It's a matter of pride to be Mexican.

94. Mexico, like no other.

95. What is made in Mexico is made well.

96. To love one's country is to love life.

Solidarity, another value under the category of justice, is defined as the ability to join with others to promote interests, responsibilities, and causes for the well-being of all. In the preschool version, obedience was the preliminary value for solidarity. Workbooks show examples of people helping other people. In a second grade workbook, following rules (illustrated as going through a maze) is the way for students to help those in need. The value of obedience is defined as the ability to face rules and norms in daily life and to respect them. The concept, however, does not include obedience to inner values, but rather to external rules, encouraging unquestioned loyalty rather than reflection. Thus solidarity, in the Values Program, seems to involve a collective connection not to one another but to a top-down unified vision.

QUESTIONNAIRES ON NATIONALISM

To find out more about how those on the border think about nationalism, we showed our videotape at public schools in both El Paso and Juárez, in university settings, including colleges of education and at educational conferences. We asked audiences to complete a brief questionnaire before viewing the tape and a longer one afterward.[97] One of the questions read, "What is good citizenship for children?" Juárez responses were clearly and consistently more nationalistic. El Paso responses were more vague and varied, with multiple messages such as individuality, being good, and good attendance.

Mexican audiences reported a more traditional and schooled notion of citizenship, focusing on a classic sense of nationalism. Over 50 percent of the responses cited patriotism and respect for national symbols: the flag, the national emblem—the eagle on a cactus with a snake in its claw—and the national anthem. Another 20 percent identified nationalism with good citizenship. Only two warned against excessive or fanatic nationalism. A teacher-training director in Juárez said he would prefer a more "tempered irreverence" toward national symbols. He appreciated that those in the United States could wear the

---

97. We collected approximately 300 questionnaires.

colors of the flag, even on their underwear if they wanted, and they could publicly joke about the president. He told how street vendors in Mexico City, selling Halloween masks of the president, were detained by the police and had their masks confiscated. "In Mexico," he said, "you don't criticize the president, he's like the nation's dad, and the Virgin of Guadalupe, she is like the mom—you are obligated to respect them both."

Besides the traditional patriotism, Juárez respondents used more affective language; for example, they commonly use the word "love" (*querer* and *amar*) with regard to their country. We noted in these Spanish-language responses that respondents frequently used the possessive form my, her, his, (*mi, su*) rather than neutral articles like "the" (*el, la*) when referring to one's country and heritage.

In contrast, the El Paso respondents had broader, more diverse definitions of citizenship. In response to the same question on citizenship for children, the majority evoked traditional themes of nationalism, while a sizable minority evoked themes of individual character and civility in behavior toward others. A little over one-third mentioned the theme of patriotism and respect for national symbols, like the flag. Obedience to authority, getting along, and good manners were infrequently mentioned. Even fewer mentioned civic responsibility, respecting self, and cooperation. Very few brought up pride in self and one's country, obedience to authority, knowledge of government history, or tools for civic engagement. In the El Paso responses we noted that citizenship was sometimes connected with work, defined as being part of the workforce, working with others in productive ways, and developing a work ethic. From this perspective, notions of good citizenship seem to reinforce marketplace effectiveness, merging nationalism with our economic system.

Many respondents from both countries define citizenship education in terms related to character and civility. Values such as good behavior, good manners, and morals were common to both El Paso and Juárez respondents. Specific behaviors included caring, sharing, and respecting others. In the last quarter of the twentieth century, school curricula have emphasized multiculturalism and respect for diversity.

Respondents' comments seem to underline an interpretation of citizenship that is open to differences and self-respect. This perspective stresses individualism and affirms pride in one's ethnic heritage.

A Mexican respondent, comparing nationalism in El Paso and Juárez wrote, "We have it and you don't." Another said that the United States "does not have much nationalism, but in Mexico, it's a matter of honor." El Paso respondents also recognized this with nostalgia: "Never forget your country" and "Believe in your country," they counseled. However, in Mexico, nationalism is associated with neither right- nor left-wing ideologues, nor with a conservative government, but with a noble, occasionally tragic history and culture. In the United States love of one's country is often merged with patriotic zeal and support for a conservative government administration and international dominance.[98]

CIVICS ON THE BORDER

While nationalism and civics are taught in both Mexico and the United States, nationalism becomes more international at the border. Here crossing is continuous; radio and television commercial and musical messages promote regional, individualist, and consumer values in Spanish, English, and a mix of the two. Juarenses[99] often yearn for a culture that is more culturally pure, that is, Mexican. Juárez teachers lamented that their city was "typically border," that is, significantly influenced by the United States. At an elementary school on the outskirts of Juárez (far from the border) an ESL teacher and several colleagues discussed immigration from the interior of Mexico. He and his colleagues all agreed that the immigrants are much more traditionally Mexican; for example, he explained that they showed greater respect for teachers and the Mexican culture. Several complained that U.S. holidays seemed to be taking over traditional Mexican holidays.

---

98. This research analysis was completed before the September 11, 2001, attacks on the United States.

99. Juárez residents.

Anglos in El Paso often worry about the mix of U.S. and Mexican cultures, that it is not "pure" U.S. [Anglo] culture. At the same time, though, businesses, the media, and their audiences reinforce a more open notion of binational solidarity and U.S. culture where multiculturalism and multilingualism have always been the norm. An El Paso radio broadcaster speaking from this perspective announces in English, "Some people call them 'illegal aliens' . . . we call them 'new listeners.'"

Mexicans seem to be more protective of their nationality than those in El Paso, especially cognizant of the economic influence of the United States. El Paso's majority Mexican American population seems to appreciate both Mexican and U.S. heritage. The local El Paso newspaper announces *quinceañeras*,[100] along with wedding engagements and anniversaries. The fact that there are many wealthy and influential Juarenses adds a different dimension to the border, helping to maintain Spanish as a language equal in status to English.

In El Paso, many Mexican traditions and holidays are celebrated and children can enroll in *folklórico* dance classes after school. Mariachi bands are part of some high school music curricula and are common in schools. Many churches have Spanish services and mariachi masses for occasions like *el día de la Virgin de Guadalupe* and *Misa de Gallo*.[101] Children celebrate Halloween at home, and they even dress in costumes at schools, but, increasingly, shrines are assembled at some schools to honor the deceased on the Day of the Dead in both cities.

We observed a Nicolas Bravo fourth and fifth grade ESL class learning a song with U.S. nationalist undercurrent. As vocabulary-building activity, English students were learning "Tie a Yellow Ribbon," a song revived periodically when veterans have returned from war, from Vietnam to the Persian Gulf. Juárez students had written the words to the song in their notebooks, discussed the meaning, and were now singing it along with the instructor. El Paso students and educa-

---

100. Debutante parties for girls on their fifteenth birthday.

101. Christmas Eve midnight mass.

TABLE 1. MOST IMPORTANT REASONS FOR A SOCIETY TO HAVE PRIMARY SCHOOLS

% of U.S. responses	% of Mexico responses
Make children self-reliant 24%	Good start academically 25%
Good start academically 19%	Make children self-reliant 22%
Start road to citizenship 16%	Start road to citizenship 20%
Experience in group 14%	Experience in group 16%

TABLE 2. MOST IMPORTANT THINGS FOR CHILDREN TO LEARN IN PRIMARY SCHOOL

% of U.S. responses	% of Mexico responses
Cooperation/Part of Group 17%	Cooperation/Part of Group 21%
Reading & Math skills 16%	Self-reliance 18%
Self-reliance 14%	Individual creativity 14%
Communication skills 14%	Reading & Math skills 11%
Problem solving 12%	Equality among diverse people 9%
Individual creativity 11%	Problem solving 7%

TABLE 3. MOST IMPORTANT CHARACTERISTICS OF ELEMENTARY SCHOOL TEACHERS

% of U.S. responses	% of Mexico responses
Knows subject matter 18%	Knows subject matter 23%
Devoted/conscientious 18%	Understands/likes children 17%
Tolerant/treats children equally 14%	Devoted/conscientious 10%
Understands/likes children 14%	Creative 8%

tors who watched the video chuckled at the irony of that song's use at an ESL class in Juárez.

How should schools go about teaching nationalism for more genuine democracy, as opposed to just learning *about* democracy? We share here what our research participants thought about schooling and democracy. Before showing our videotape, we asked viewers to complete a short survey on three items: (1) the most important reasons for a society to have primary schools, (2) the most important things for children to learn in primary school, and (3) the most important characteristics of elementary school teachers. These do not necessarily represent all borderlanders, but they can illustrate differences (or lack of national difference) at the El Paso–Juárez border. The tables on page 71 show the responses.

Table 1 illustrates a great deal of similarity between views from both sides of the border. The much-vaunted distinction between individualism and communalism in sociopsychological literature is muted. Similar percentages of respondents cite self-reliance (almost a quarter listing this in the top three), and group experience is cited less in both countries, but on the Mexico side, the academic start emerges on top.

In Table 2, some intriguing differences emerge. For both sides of the border, the importance of cooperation and becoming a group member emerges at the top, but more strongly for the Mexico respondents. Below that, slightly different weights are found for different values, merging the supposed contrasts of both sides.

Table 3 shows similarity across both sides of the border. Knowledge of subject matter emerges supreme, especially in Mexico, while personal characteristics and understanding of children follow thereafter.

CONCLUSION

Children are exposed to civic education from their earliest days in school. Students can learn a national identity in school, but how that serves them as adults is not certain. Civic and values education can prepare children for adult interaction and engagement in democracy. It can open up relevant knowledge about society, government, and people, and it can stir the curiosity in and desire to connect with others over civic matters. It can provide opportunities for exercising responsibility and tools to solve problems, as individuals or as group members.

The connection among civic education, democracy, and nationalism creates interesting patterns on the border. Much of what is judged to be civic education consists of an effort to instill pride in nation, patriotism and loyalty, obedience to laws, and memorization of details and facts based on a more conservative construction of history. Teachers on both sides of the border are very concerned that students not just repeat but understand these national concepts.

Children in Juárez schools are taught specific lessons on citizenship and culture consistently. Both El Paso and Juárez viewers of the video corroborated our remarks about Mexico's patriotic themes that engender love of country. Children in El Paso schools learn a mix of ideas and emotions that are bundled together as patriotic: service, good behavior, and Texas pride. The issue of democracy and civic education is complicated by the multicultural nature of the border society, involving power relations that privilege some, but that often exclude non-mainstream citizens.

Schools supposedly prepare children for citizenship and democracy through civic education, which can include lessons, processes, and activities, and campus values that support the appearance of the democratic process. But the formal democracy taught in schools can differ drastically from grassroots, inclusive, democratic practices.

Many of the children in this study live in families that have been at the margins of, or even outside of, the democratic life that both countries claim to practice. Their parents work at minimum wage levels or slightly above. Others, from both El Paso and Juárez, come from middle-class families with parents who are professionals. Their engagement with democratic institutions is invoked periodically during elections. For the children, civic education is a coherent part of the curriculum. It is usually discussed as a topic in social studies classes or on pseudo-democratic occasions like voting for party food, yet it is pervasive in everyday classroom life.

CHAPTER 4

Classroom Organization and School Management: Lessons in Civics

"Being a good citizen at school is like being a good citizen when you grow up . . . following the rules is like following laws later." (Principal, Vilas Elementary School, talking to students at a school assembly)

The connection between obedience (following rules) and citizenship is complex. Students need to understand and obey rules, just as communities need to agree on and obey laws for their collective safety and well-being. But often teachers and administrators expect passive acquiescence to rules rather than an active exchange in the creation or reformation of rules. This is represented by the way teachers manage their classrooms, in whether they allow students freedom of movement, for example, or expect them to stay in their seats at all times. While passivity and conformity make teaching easier and often serve as proxies for good behavior, do they teach good citizenship? This chapter shows some of the different ways teachers in El Paso and Juárez strive to create learning environments that balance order and freedom.

We enter a Juárez special needs classroom in full swing. Three groups, each with four students, are working on a sentence sequencing activity, cutting apart strips of scrambled words: *con . . . Yo . . . hablo . . .*

Photo by Sara Guerrero-Rippberger

Collaboration, Juárez classroom.

amigos . . . mis.[102] They will rearrange the words and glue them in order into their notebooks. Working socially, they share glue, read the words out loud to each other, and discuss the possibilities for sentences, dropping scraps of paper on the floor. They lean on each other, reaching to get dabs of glue or borrow an eraser. A girl gently swats a boy on the arm during the discussion and he smiles. Personal space seems close in this classroom. Another boy puts his arm around a girl's head, his hand resting on her ponytail and she doesn't protest. The teacher walks from group to group asking students to read their finished product to her, "*Yo hablo con mis amigos.*" She pats them on the head and says "*muy bien,*" or works with them, if they have put the words together wrong.

As the teacher, Ms. Flores,[103] calls out to them to change activities, a boy gets up without being asked, takes a broom from the back of the room, and starts to sweep up the scraps of paper on the floor. Two girls soon join him in sweeping, others spontaneously bring them trash from their desks and toss it into the dust pile. Toward the end, the teacher

102. with . . . I . . . talk . . . friends . . . my

103. All teachers' names are pseudonyms.

asks an older girl to finish the sweeping while the rest of the class goes on to the next lesson. There appears to be a free-form flow to the lessons with the teacher guiding children through the activities.

In an El Paso monolingual first grade social studies class, we observe an interesting parallel lesson—on responsibility and cleaning up. The teacher, Ms. Jansen, explains the value of all work, from school janitor to president of the United States She points out how the janitor helps us keep our school clean, and then asks, "Who else is responsible for helping our school to stay clean?" Students offered suggestions, "the gardeners," "the principal," "teachers," and to each she responds, "Yes, but who *else*?" Finally a little boy says, "Everybody," to which she responds emphatically, "Yes! It is *every*body's responsibility." But students in this class do not clean the room nor do they leave their seats without permission. The only time we saw students cleaning up was when they were asked to put their books and materials away before recess, and it was just their own space they cleaned.

Schools are places where children learn not only academics but also culturally appropriate behavior. Organizational and management strategies reveal underlying cultural rules and regulations that teachers often tacitly and sometimes unknowingly reinforce. In and outside of classrooms, teachers and students interact in ways that exercise civic behavior. The opening drama illustrates this point. El Paso students and teachers value the concept of cleaning up and responsibility, but rarely are children asked or volunteer to take responsibility for cleaning up during class time. Juárez students, on the other hand, spontaneously put into practice the ideal.

The importance of understanding tacit expectations in schools cannot be underestimated. To bring these to the surface and examine them helps educators become more reflective, and thus more effective. Within schools, organization and management of classrooms, such as seating arrangements, discipline, social relationships, uniforms, and time, show what is valued in classrooms and in society.

Schools in El Paso and Juárez, on the surface, have obvious similarities, such as experiential, hands-on learning, thematic units, assertive discipline plans, preponderance of women teaching in the lower grades, and a common ethnic heritage. The differences, often subtle, illustrate some of the ways our border cities look at values and education through different lenses. Personal space, time, individual and collaborative behavior, and reward systems illustrate some of the less obvious differences we have for civic training.

PERSONAL SPACE AND WARMTH

At the early grade levels, children in the Juárez schools were playful and showed more personal and emotional attachment with their teachers. We saw children come up to hug the teachers or whisper in their ear about the need to use the restroom. Juárez teachers move freely around their classrooms, in group-based activities, attending to individuals and groups. The teacher of the special needs classroom at Benito Juárez School walked around comfortably, chatting informally after she assigned tasks. A first grade class at the same school seemed almost chaotic, with the intensive student-student and teacher-student interaction.

At Benito Juárez School, we observed this closeness and informality in two classrooms, one of them a first grade room with thirty-five children and the other a "special needs" class of approximately twenty students aged six to thirteen, with different needs, some emotional, some academic, and some motivational. The special needs class was staffed by a teacher, a social worker, and the school psychologist.

This special needs classroom is brightly decorated, but not overwhelming. Flowers, numbers, the alphabet, and an Instituto Federal Electoral civic education poster adorn the walls. The class is arranged in three rows of bench-type desks, each desk seating two to three children. Students move freely, standing up when they want, looking over each other's work, and commenting. A younger boy does a pirouette in the front of the room, unscolded. The teacher introduces a story using pictures, about a boy who rides his bicycle to the store. There are lots of interaction and most of the students seem interested, excited even, calling out answers, raising their hands, and leaning forward on their benches. The teacher asks them to raise their hands, which they do obediently, but they continue to call out answers. They discuss the pictures, the sequence of events, and they write words and sentences on the board. Children approach the teacher to ask for permission to go to the restroom (outside the room); she nods and adds, "*correle*."[104] A group of four students return from speech therapy and take their seats blending with the class without interrupting.

For a follow-up practice activity to the reading lesson, the teacher and an older girl fill bottle caps with glue from a gallon glue container. Students copy off the board into their own notebooks, drawing pictures to illustrate the story. The teacher walks by each student checking her/his work, handing each some glue and a long strip of paper with words from the story that they will cut apart and glue into their notebooks under the sentences they have written.

As the activity draws to a close, Ms. Flores calls out, "Hands on your head, hands on your ears, hands on your nose," to get their attention. Students respond by putting their hands on their heads, ears, and mouths. The teacher continues until she has all their attention, hands no longer on the previous task, and minds ready to pay attention to instructions for the next activity.

She asks the children to group themselves in four teams, each with four students. They go about creating the teams, grouping themselves, noisy and social; a girl pulls a boy over to her group; he shrugs but comes along happily. Their task is to put ten beans in a little plastic bag, close it with a rubber band, and put ten of these bags in a box (illustrating place value: ones—single beans, tens—plastic bags of ten beans, and hundreds—boxes of ten bags). The teacher had collected bulk candy boxes from shops in the area, and brought the other materials, beans, baggies, and rubber bands, from home. The children work cooperatively, discussing, counting, and recounting beans. At the front of the room, the social worker works with about four students who are still learning to count. They use a cardboard box painted with ten big dots; the students put a bean on each dot, counting as they do. They count each bean again as they take it off the dot and put it in a plastic

---

104. Hurry.

Bean math project, Juárez classroom.

bag. Learning is comfortable, informal, and social. The classroom management style shows a value for individual freedom and a relaxed, natural setting.

Two classrooms down, an afternoon first grade classroom follows up on a reading lesson. The learning environment is quite different, but personal interaction is still close and intense. The teacher, Ms. Moreno, pushes the students' individual desks together with the students still in their desks, creating four learning groups. Students are not asked to work cooperatively, but they consult the teacher and one another on their individual seatwork. One group cuts out pictures from newspapers to glue into their notebooks, illustrating the story the teacher had just read. Another group practices making letter shapes; the other two read from their workbook and write short answers.

To an outsider, it looks like the first group is made up of the less mature children (mixed gender), who try to do the work but are not very accurate. Another group (three boys, one girl) chat and giggle, not accomplishing much at all. A third group, all girls, work diligently and do fairly well. The last group, all girls again, do all the written work, quickly, quietly, and accurately. Ms. Moreno later explained that she had grouped the class according to a syllabic method, based on Piaget's stages of learning. The first two groups, she told us, are the pre-syllabic, who do not know letters yet, but draw circles and lines as preparation for writing letters. The third and fourth groups are the syllabic groups and the readers.

El Paso educators who watched this class on the video expressed concern about noise levels and student movement. "Shh!" one said, reacting to the background noise in the video. Some asked what the lessons were all about in the Juárez classrooms. One El Paso teacher, seeing the large classrooms in Juárez, gasped, "thirty-two kids and no helpers!?" Teachers were surprised that the students in Juárez can walk up to the teacher during the class to "distract" her, in their words. Everyone, they said, seemed to be doing something different, "Is it a lesson?" a teacher asked.

Regarding chaos, a graduate education student commented how the rooms in Juárez are noisy, but that it probably is "learning noise: kids working in groups, helping each other, discussing the project, to get the job done." Class size, rapid growth of the city, and meager resources in Juárez may also contribute to the sociability of students where they share school supplies and space, often three to a desk. A Juárez teacher explained the necessity of "making do," "de la nada, sacamos bastante."[105]

An El Paso graduate student who had gone to primary school in Juárez explained that you need to be social to survive in Mexico, to share everything with your companions. Another graduate student commented on the waste of supplies and materials in the United States, and, in contrast, the scarcity in Juárez. He told us, "U.S. kids don't appreciate what they are getting. If they had to pay for pencils, photocopies, etc. like the Mexican kids, they might be more appreciative."

Students in a graduate seminar on education at the University of Texas at El Paso, many of whom were Mexican American, viewed the video and found the concept of personal space particularly interesting. They saw personal space in the United States defined so precisely

---

105. We do a lot with nothing, that is, we are very creative.

because students need to fit into what they called a "capitalist model" as a piece of the machinery, "you need to fit into your place in the world of jobs." Another added that the personal space resembled the cubicles of the comic strip "Dilbert," where people are kept separate and isolated from one another for the purposes of productivity.

A Juárez director mentioned that even the architecture of the school and placement of classrooms and playgrounds tend to nurture certain kinds of behavior and activity. El Paso schools have very few informal central meeting places, although auditoriums and administration offices can serve as common ground. El Paso schools usually separate children to supervised side or rear playgrounds for recess, while most of the Juárez schools have a patio or courtyard in the center of the school for children and adults. Mexican architecture seems to offer more settings for informal mingling of children and adults.

Somehow classroom management changes from more chaotic (or free, depending on one's perspective) arrangements in earlier grades to more organized behavior in later grades. When we observed Juárez fourth grade students and older, we saw contrasts with the earlier years, from students who enjoyed interaction and play to students sitting in lines and rows and focusing on the teacher. These students on the whole were very respectful of teachers when they were present, perhaps the result of more ordered and individualistic classroom expectations.

At Nicolas Bravo, we visited an ESL lesson, where we heard an impromptu lecture on being responsible for your own work. The regular fifth grade teacher sits at her desk, while the itinerant ESL teacher leads a vocabulary lesson. Forty-two students sit at the bench-like desks, two to a desk. Mr. Avila walks up and down the rows of students inspecting their homework. For those who have the work done, he says, "*Bien*," but for those who do not, he explains to them quietly, "*Es el problema, si no traemos tarea, no podemos avanzar.*"[106] He walks to the chalkboard and writes, "*T/F*," explaining, that there are two types of people, "*triumfadores y fracasados.*"[107] He asks them enthusiastically,

---

106. This is a problem, if we don't do our homework, we cannot advance.

107. winners and losers.

Group work, math project, Juárez school.

"Which do we want to be?" to which they happily call out, "Winners!" He does not single anyone out, but he tells them, "We teachers don't baby sit, and we are not here to scold you. No, we are here to help you learn and enjoy learning." He then encourages them to study hard and learn all they can.

At Revolución School, we visited another upper grade elementary classroom. The director takes us to a fifth grade classroom where an ESL lesson is going on. Desks are in rows and a travel poster and a map of the world with Mexico in the center are taped to the wall. When invited to speak with us, students greeted us in English, "Good morning," "How are you?" "What is your name?" We respond, and ask them similar questions, "My name is Susan, how about you, what is your name?" We stay about twenty minutes, interacting with the students and teachers, and then move on to visit other classrooms. Students stay in their desks and interact with us politely, happy to be able to practice their English on native speakers.

In many El Paso elementary classrooms, even when students were participating actively, we observed a more orderly environment.

Teachers and students seemed comfortable with, or at least tolerant of, a more controlled environment. For the most part, students are serious, sitting in their places, and raising their hands if they wish to comment or ask questions. In later grades, enthusiasm often wanes.

Ms. Jansen's first grade monolingual class at Schuster is a high-intensity experience. As students enter the room after recess, the teacher tells each of them, "Go to your seat." They talk loudly and she hushes them as they sit down around a long rectangular table. The teacher leads the lesson on responsibility and cleaning up, related at the beginning of this chapter. Students respond to her individually when they are called on.

While teachers in both cities are varied—many very warm and caring, others less so—most video viewers commented on the closer, more affectionate relationship between students and teachers in Juárez, and in El Paso bilingual classes with Mexican American teachers. Juárez teachers use affectionate terms with their students, like daughter or son (*hija/o*), they touch more, and they make requests more personal, for example, "Put the date on the paper *for me*." Several Juárez teachers noticed that the Mexican students appear to be more comfortable approaching teachers. Several observed what they called a "barrier that students did not pass" in El Paso schools that indicated to them a greater distance between students and teachers.

A second grade bilingual classroom we visited at Schuster had only nine students. Video viewers commented frequently that this bilingual class (and others) seemed to have a warmer, more family-like atmosphere. Nine computers lined one of the walls; other walls were covered with student work, a copy of the U.S. Constitution, and math tables. The teacher, Ms. Guerrero, had the students working in small groups on a math project measuring distances around the room. The noise level was low, as she moved from student to student, speaking to them in Spanish about their work.

The atmosphere was harmonious, more like a family working on homework than a formalized teacher-led presentation. Making a transition from the measuring project to P.E., the teacher explains calmly, quietly, "You will be going to P.E. soon, but when you come back you will have about ten minutes to finish your work. She never raises her voice or asks students for their attention—they seem to be in tune with her, listening and calmly responding when she talks. When they are ready to leave for P.E., she excuses them quietly, "Table one may go; table two, thank you for waiting so patiently, you may go." When they return, they quietly go back to measuring the classroom floor plan in inches.

In a Vilas bilingual first grade classroom we observed an activity that involved the whole class in a reading comprehension lesson. Students were active, happy, and orderly. The class had fifteen students, a teacher, and a teacher's assistant. Led by the Mexican American teacher, Ms. Gunther, students acted out a story they had just read, about a farmer who plants a beet that grows so big it is almost impossible to pull up. The farmer gets help from her husband, the household cat, and a host of farmyard animals. As Ms. Gunther reads the story out loud, the students act out their part. A boy plays the beet, standing and stretching from a crouching position to show how he grows from a tiny seed to a huge red beet. A girl plays the farmer tending the beet, and later trying to pull it out of the ground. All students take part, one by one, holding on to the waist of the student in front of them, helping to pull the beet out of the ground. They call out the refrain, "But the beet would not come up!" each time a new character is added to the line. Eventually the beet comes up, but not until everyone in the classroom gets into the line and helps pull. El Paso and Juárez classrooms are similar in the types of interactive, theme-based lessons, and they vary in organization, but each reinforces cultural expectations of children and of appropriate learning environments.

TIME

While we saw differences in space, time, and individual and collective behavior, time stood out prominently to us. Even at the earliest grade levels, we observed intriguing differences in the prominence of clocks and their meaning. In El Paso, many children wore wristwatches; we saw a clock in every classroom and often in the halls, and we observed many lessons based around telling time. Clocks were used as a basis for activities like counting by fives, estimating, and pie graphs. Teachers proceeded according to lesson plans, to accommodate policies dictating the number of minutes per subject. At particular times of the day, students formed lines to exit the classroom for art enrichment classes, for lunch in the school cafeteria, or for group trips to the restrooms. El Paso teachers watching the video and commenting on this sense of time and order told how common it was to hear each other saying, "come on; you're wasting time" or "OK, get ready; I'm counting down the seconds it takes you to get back to your seats . . . 30, 29, 28, etc." Another agreed, "We are so time-oriented," then parodying herself in a mock "teacher" voice she said, "You have 30 seconds to get back to your seat." Teachers, too, are under time pressures, submitting weekly lesson plans in time frames to principals. They expressed relief, though, that things were not like the "old days" when supervisors might reprimand them if they ran five minutes over a timed lesson plan in their plan book. Student teachers are taught the importance of "time on task" in their teacher preparation courses, showing the value placed on productivity and efficiency.

By contrast, in the Juárez classrooms we visited, there was rarely a clock on the wall, and very few students wore wristwatches; the teacher was usually the only one in the classroom with a watch. In only two or three elementary classrooms did we observe a clock on the wall, and this was brought in by the teacher as a decoration as much as a timepiece. We heard no references to minutes, and children were allowed to decide when they needed to use the restroom. Teachers seemed to pace lessons with the flow of the class. Students in El Paso stayed in their seats much more, and they were more distant from the teacher and us as visitors. At one point, in a monolingual class, when a student asked to go to the restroom, the teacher told him, "We don't go to the restroom until the lesson is over," then added, "Unless it's an emergency."

In Juárez schools, bells announcing class and recess are rung at approximate (rather than exact) times, when the principal feels it is appropriate. Teachers respond to bells dismissing students soon thereafter, as they bring their work to a close before running out to play. In the United States, teachers usually follow a schedule based on distinct time frames. If bells are used, they are often on a timer set to go off at exact times, whether appropriate to the lesson or not. On many occasions, we saw U.S. students shove their unfinished work in their desk and rush out to recess at the sound of the recess bell. Upon viewing Juárez schools in the videotapes, El Paso educators worried about the efficient use of time. In Juárez, we saw first and second grade students arriving late to class without censure; in El Paso, after the bell rang, tardiness is recorded, and penalized if excessive.

We saw very few calendars in Juárez classrooms, although primary teachers occasionally started written assignments by having students write the date at the top of their papers. U.S. primary teachers frequently start the day with a group discussion based on the calendar date, day of the week, season, and sometimes weather—all of which provides training to think in terms of time and cycles.

In one sense, the emphasis on time seemed excessive in El Paso classrooms, particularly in the lower grades. The concern with order and efficiency did not fit together with the natural flow of learning. However, teachers are laying the foundation for life in a society and workplace in which people, more and more, are expected to manage time efficiently, and be relentlessly productive.

As we observed classroom interaction and organization, we noticed that both human relationships and notions of time are important to people in Juárez and El Paso, but that frequently they played a unique role. In El Paso, time, punctuality, and clock-driven agendas seem to take precedence over personal contact and human relations. Juárez, by contrast, while valuing both time and people, placed human relationships and a more organic flow of activities above time. Even though both cities clearly influence each other, and they have a similar history and people, divergent national attitudes are prominent in the classrooms.

In Juárez, people and human relationships are very important. On several occasions in Juárez schools, we watched as a teacher spent her recess and part of class time talking with parents, with us, or with other teachers. On other occasions, teachers left their classes to introduce us

Photo by Susan Rippberger

Classroom organization, Juárez school.

to the principal or guide us around the school. Children often approached us during class to greet us, give us a hug, sit on our lap, or ask us to "say something in English." Once, when we apologized to the teacher for disrupting her class, she explained that it was okay, that the children would find someone else to talk to if we weren't there.

Cultural norms of time and relationships affect teaching in each city, which in turn tends to reinforce these cultural norms. Where teachers place greater emphasis on schedules than on students, people, or learning projects, the learning style seems to promote efficiency and productivity. In Juárez, learning is built more on concepts of social discourse and interaction in lower grades, and it is based on more of an obedience model in upper grades. These differing models of efficiency (based on time) and sociability (based on relationships) have an impact on the learning process in each country and how people are expected to interact as adults.

El Paso schools, while efficient and productive, do have engaging activities for children. At Schuster, for example, we observed school-wide participatory reading activities that went along with national holidays. During a pre-Thanksgiving week visit, teachers had organized students into three groups based on the traditional U.S. Thanksgiving story: the Pilgrims, the Mayflowers, and the Native Americans. Another visit was on National Reading Day. Teachers, teacher aids, and a few students dressed in their favorite book characters—Robin Hood, Tom Sawyer, and a Pink Power Ranger. During these times, classroom behavior was more relaxed.

INDIVIDUALITY OR CONFORMITY

While U.S. culture is often considered to place greater emphasis on individuality, schools require greater conformity and control, limiting individual behavior. Students must be supervised at all times, and they are increasingly held accountable to state and national standards via high-stakes testing. Interestingly, uniforms in El Paso symbolize conformity more than group identity.

Uniforms in Mexico, long a requirement for public and private schools, were viewed as a sign of belonging. Currently, many schools in El Paso have instituted school uniform policies. Probably a majority of parents support such a policy, with the rationale that it costs less, creates order, and reduces the need to negotiate about and make exceptions to "appropriate" clothing in the school dress codes. Students and some parents worry that free expression and individuality are lost in the move toward conformity in dress. Several teachers insisted that the purpose for uniforms is to eliminate baggy clothing[108] ("that could conceal a weapon"), and gang colors.

Juárez teachers and school directors are usually flexible about enforcing uniform policies for parents of limited means. In El Paso, students have less leeway; all must wear uniforms, and with shirts tucked in. Juárez students often identify with their school colors. When we showed Juárez students our videotapes, they were surprised to see that some public schools in El Paso did not require uniforms.

---

108. What administrators saw as "baggy clothing" was, to the students, the "hip-hop" look, a popular style across the United States.

Photo by Susan Rippberger

Friends in uniform at recess, Juárez school.

They asked us, "How can other people identify where you go to school?" Here the student's social identity is built into their educational experience more than in El Paso.

CONCLUSION

In these border schools, students spend much of their day in surroundings that send continuous civic cues about what is valued and rewarded. School organization and its rewards and penalties mesh closely with grand, long-term preparations for work, social life, and consumption as adults.

In El Paso classrooms, students learn order and time efficiency at a very early age. Individualism is stressed more than community, yet conformity is stressed over individualistic behavior. Juárez teachers tend to nurture a collectivity or community, but they also allow more chaotic or independent behavior in the classroom and on the playground. This often has the appearance of letting "kids be kids." In Juárez, social interaction is extensive in the earlier grades, though orderly classrooms emerge in later years.

Local settings—schools and classrooms—as well are teachers and activities on the surface resemble each other in many ways, yet they manifest interesting contrasts in areas that are often stereotyped but not as often examined. Concepts such as time, social and individual behavior, organization and management strategies take on subtle differences within each city's schools. This is especially significant in these two border cities. Most observers consider El Paso to have a strong Mexican influence and Juárez to have a strong U.S. influence, yet both seem to maintain culturally specific mores for classroom behavior.

Cultural stereotypes of individualistic and collective behavior can be complicated at the border. National and cultural mixes occur with the continuous short- and long-term border crossing. Recent developments on social and cooperative learning strategies are causing schools in both countries to become more collectively organized for social engagement. While it may be tempting to classify students, cities, and nations into static notions of culture, lived experience is much more complex.

CHAPTER 5
Bilingualism: Language Policy and Use

In standard English, a rich baritone, male radio voice announces the call letters for an El Paso–based, bilingual radio station: "K-B-N-A . . . feel free to speak in any language."

In contrast to this happy invitation to speak in any language, many Mexican Americans speaking Spanish in public places tell of being admonished: "Speak English, this is America." This *is* America, where freedom of speech is protected by the Constitution, and multilingual communities of immigrants are the foundation of the nation. In the El Paso–Juárez region, immigration and bilingualism are the norm. Yet unwritten norms of language, regulated by power and class, show what we value about language and national identity. Formal language policy and informal usage, though, are often contradictory.

In this chapter, we examine political, legal, and social issues surrounding language use and how these are translated into specific language practices in El Paso and Juárez schools that prepare students to interact comfortably in a binational setting. Here bilingualism is a necessity, not just an enriching option, reinforcing one's own sense of national pride, and at the same time, reinforcing binationalism.

LANGUAGE AND NATIONAL IDEOLOGY

Official language policy in both Mexico and the United States focuses on national unity and language purity via the language of the dominant social/political group. But actual language usage varies depending on what is appropriate for the specific setting and event. While English has always been accepted as the official language, the United States is multilingual. In certain areas English is not the common unifying language. In Little Havana, Florida, or downtown El Paso, for instance, more Spanish than English is spoken. Spanish television and radio programming from both Mexico and the United States cater to these Spanish-speaking populations.

In El Paso, privilege in hiring goes to bilingual people in social service agencies such as police, hospitals, and schools, so that employees can communicate with the majority of their clients. Businesses, too, are quick to adapt to a bilingual society. McDonald's, in Spanish-speaking areas throughout the southwest, makes sure even monolingual English–speaking employees know how to ask if customers want their *papas* to be *chicas o grandes*.[109] This is not just a U.S. phenomenon. U.S. retirement communities in Mexico, for example, are often monolingual English and in Mennonite areas in Mexico, German is the common language. In these situations the context rather than official language policy dictates which language unifies the community, and whose national identity is valued.

Currently in the United States, Latinos make up about 12 percent of the nation's population, with nearly 32 million concentrated in California, Florida, Texas, New York, New Jersey, and Illinois. Of this diverse group, up to 20 million are of Mexican heritage, 3 million of whom migrate back and forth between Mexico and the United States.[110] Their presence and political clout are important to both the U.S. and the Mexican governments. During the 2000 presidential elections, the main Mexican candidates, Fox and Cárdenas, valued the

---

109. large or small french fries.

110. John Ward Anderson, "Politicians without Borders: Mexico's Candidates Court Support for Migrants in U.S.," *Washington Post*, May 9, 2000, A20.

"American Mexicans" living in the United States enough to campaign
in cities with large Mexican American communities. The candidates
promised to work for fewer immigration restrictions and a human
rights agenda.

Politicians in the United States, too, must take the growing Latino
population and their language needs seriously, not just in token political recognition. "Don't take us for granted. And don't patronize us with
a few throw away sentences in Spanish. Deliver on our issues," reports
a California newspaper in a Mexican American community.[111] Latino
politicians struggle to regain and reclaim their heritage, some attending intensive summer programs in Mexico for both linguistic and cultural renewal. This must be gratifying and surprising to their parents'
generation, who were often forbidden to speak Spanish in school, even
during recess. It may even be surprising to the parents who encouraged
their children to speak English to avoid the pain and isolation they
experienced as children. This has significance for a nation such as the
United States that has valued the English language as a unifying agent,
and for Mexico that has valued Spanish for the same purpose. How do
community changes such as these affect nationalistic concepts of language purity? How do bilingual and border practices influence mainstream values?

Language adaptation and invention occur in bilingual settings.
Code switching[112] in El Paso and using borrowed words in Juárez are
very common. Often Mexican Americans in the southwest code switch
as a sign of cultural identity, and as evidence of a border patois. For
example, radio stations, like KBNA—*Que Buena*,[113] or KNTE—*La
Caliente*,[114] regularly mix languages in their announcements, "*más* food,
less *dinero*,"[115] says a restaurant advertisement. Another station, brag-

---

111. *Orange County Resister*, May 8, 2000.

112. Going back and forth between two languages.

113. How nice.

114. The hot one.

115. More food for less money.

ging that they are the only bilingual radio station, asserts, "*más y más gente*[116] are listening to *La Caliente*." These stations play both Latin and U.S. pop music. An El Paso highway billboard promoting Mexican-made beer, as well as national and linguistic pride, points out, "*Cerveza es mejor que* beer."[117]

Although Juarenses typically do not code switch, many borrowed words have replaced standard Spanish, like troca or peek-op (for truck, instead of *camioneta)*, or fensa (for fence, instead of *cerca* or *reja)*. Other common borrowings include mapear (for *trapear*, to mop), el freeway (for *la carretera* or *el camino)*, parkiar (for *estacionar)*, post-eets (little yellow stick-on notes), and wheela (for *bicicleta)*, among others. Border languages as an expression of border cultures have an impact on national identity, where certain languages or combinations of languages take precedence over the officially sanctioned language. These language adaptations take on different meanings for school children who learn a "foreign" language in school, whether it is Spanish or English.

LANGUAGE AND SCHOOLING

Embedded in educational practices are larger concerns of national identity and government interest in civics training. Educational curriculum, as a reflection of this language debate, has never been neutral; books, pedagogy, and teaching styles all embody culture, power, class, and gender relations, privileging some, excluding others.[118]

The 2000 Census figures show that 20 percent of U.S. children (aged five to seventeen) speak a language other than English. Seventy percent of these school-aged children are Spanish speakers (up 15 percent from 1990). Yet most teachers across the United States are still being trained under the assumption that their students will be native

---

116. More and more people . . .

117. *Cerveza* is better than beer. *Cerveza* is the Spanish word for *beer.*

118. See for example, Michael W. Apple, "The Text and Cultural Politics," *Educational Researcher* (October 1992): 4–19.

speakers of English. Since teachers often lack training as language specialists, some become frustrated or even resentful that their students cannot respond to their teaching practices. This can cause teachers to lower expectations and blame students, their families, and their culture for low academic performance.

Bilingual teachers find variations of Spanish spoken by students whose school and community language can be different, even within the same language. For example, doing well on a language test may have nothing to do with the ability to communicate skillfully in different settings. An El Paso bilingual middle school teacher coached her class of immigrant students: "You may have learned to speak Spanish a certain way from your parents, or your grandparents. It's not wrong. It's your language. But you may find out that in school there is a variation of Spanish you have to learn to do well in your classes." Here the teacher recognizes and affirms the language her students use, showing them the importance of language pluralism.

In early 2000, the U.S. secretary of education pointed out the need for dual language programs in responding to the global economy and the needs of a growing Latino population. One of the advantages is that two-way bilingual programs integrate language minority and language majority students and provide both with a second language. The focus of instruction is the same core academic curriculum that students in monolingual programs experience. An intended outcome of these programs is to enhance cross-cultural understanding and appreciation.

LANGUAGE POLICY

In the United States, the 1972 landmark Supreme Court decision *Lau v. Nichols* set the precedent for bilingual education on the basis of access to curriculum. It ruled that classes taught only in English denied equal access to students who spoke other languages. Initially bilingual education was legislated as compensatory or remedial, to bring children up to par so they could compete with the native English speakers whose culture and language are aligned with that of the educational system.

In Mexico, English as a foreign language is part of the standard curriculum for middle school and above. The Mexican national curriculum for secondary (middle) school lists "*programa de inglés*" as part of a section on foreign languages (English and French are the only languages listed). The rationale stated for knowledge of foreign languages is to recognize and better appreciate one's own language and culture.[119]

Bilingual education policy for Mexico was initiated in the early 1950s as part of the newly formed national Instituto Nacional Indigenista (INI).[120] Native Mexican children received instruction and reading primers in their own language. In the introduction to the indigenous language books, the SEP quotes from the Mexican Constitution recognizing Mexico's multicultural makeup, guaranteeing the protection and development of its cultures and their languages.[121]

The Mexican Secretariat of Public Education, with other government agencies, puts out a map illustrating cultural and linguistic diversity in Mexico.[122] The map includes a list of Spanish-speaking populations outside Mexico, placing the United States as having the fifth-largest, after Mexico, Spain, Colombia, and Argentina. This shows how important the Spanish-speaking population is to Mexico as part of their extended language family and sphere of influence.

In Texas throughout the 1960s, 1970s, and 1980s, bilingual programs were developed to help language minority students succeed academically by teaching them in a language they could understand. The legislature provided for bilingual education in public schools, showing support for the large Spanish-speaking population. By the early 1970s,

---

119. *Educación Básica: Secundaria Plan y Programas de Estudio* (México, D.F.: Secretaría de Educación Pública, 1993).

120. National Indian Institute or Bureau of Indian Affairs.

121. SEP, *Bats'i K'op, Lengua Tsotsil, Chiapas, primer ciclo*, 1994.

122. Secretaría de Educación Pública, Consejo Nacional para la Cultura y las Artes, *La Diversidad Cultural de México—Los Pueblos Indígenas y sus 62 Idiomas* (México, D.F.: Secretaría de Educación Pública and Consejo Nacional para la Cultura y las Artes, 1998).

bilingual education programs were made mandatory if twenty or more students of Limited English Proficiency (LEP) were identified at a single grade level, beginning at first grade. The Texas legislature later made bilingual education mandatory in kindergarten through third grade; bilingual programs in fourth and fifth grade became optional. Through the 1980s, the bilingual curriculum was developed and expanded for grades kindergarten through fifth, and ESL was implemented in middle and high schools. This commitment to immigrants and Spanish speakers, frequently of low income, shows a national and state value in offering their children equal access to education.

TYPES OF BILINGUAL EDUCATION

There are various orientations to language programs based on underlying assumptions about what school is for and what language means. Depending on one's attitude, minority languages have been defined variably as a problem, as a right, or as a resource.[123] If language pluralism is labeled a problem, the solution is assimilation to English in the United States, or Spanish in Mexico, as soon as possible. If language pluralism is seen as a basic right, as a legitimate expression of one's cultural heritage, then it is seen as worthy for use in classroom instruction. If it is defined as a resource for a nation's economic and social advantage, or individual social mobility, then bilingualism is to be encouraged and developed in the schools for all students, not just for language minority students.[124] This is the case with the U.S. secretary of education's endorsement that all students receive dual language programs. Resources to create widespread dual language programs, however, did not accompany the endorsement.

Bilingual education has three general, but contested, purposes: (1) transitional programs, helping students move from their dominant lan-

123. Raul Yzaguirre, "What's the Fuss? Rethinking Schools," *Urban Educational Journal* 13 (winter 1998–99): 8.

124. Richard Ruiz, "Orientations in Language Planning," *NABE: Journal for the National Association for Bilingual Education* 8 (1984): 15–34.

guage to English only, (2) maintenance programs, maintaining Spanish while adding English, and (3) enrichment programs, an extension of maintenance programs, including two-way language programs.

Transitional educational programs in the United States, often seen as remedial, help children switch from the language they have learned at home to English as quickly as possible. This is often at the expense of the development of vocabulary and thinking skills in their first language (most often Spanish). In Mexico transitional language programs are found in indigenous schools where Spanish replaces native Mexican languages. In both countries, these programs are largely assimilation campaigns.

Ideally, U.S. students are moved out of bilingual programs when they are able to succeed in an English learning environment. In one El Paso school district, criteria for moving students from a bilingual program include passing the language arts portion of the state standardized test, a parent's request, and/or if the language spoken at home changes to English. The number making the change from bilingual classes to English-only has gradually risen from about 14 percent in 1992 to about 40 percent in 1995. In Mexican rural areas, bilingual education typically runs through elementary school,[125] depending on the availability of teachers and other resources. Indigenous students who want to continue their education must move to an urban area where all instruction is given in Spanish.

Maintenance programs, on the other hand, acknowledge the importance of the child's family language and culture, *adding* a second language (English in the United States) rather than *eliminating* the first language. Dual-language programs team up monolingual English-speaking teachers with bilingual Spanish/English-speaking teachers to work with bilingual groups of students. The outcome is to make all students competent in both languages. Frequently the teacher

---

125. Until the 1990s, indigenous bilingual schools typically offered only grades one and two. Primary education is now expanding through sixth grade as infrastructure reaches rural areas. This in itself illustrates the belated national value and support of nonmainstream cultures and languages.

who speaks English learns some Spanish, too. In Mexico dual language programs are typically enrichment programs for middle- and upper-income students attending private schools. These are native Spanish speakers who want to learn a second language such as English, French, or German.

Unfortunately, lack of funding or follow-through, severely limited bilingual materials, and an insufficient number of truly bilingual teachers have always inhibited the full potential of public school bilingual programs in both the United States and Mexico. Typically, bilingual teachers care very much about their students and want them to succeed, but they do not always receive the support they need in terms of specific training, appropriate materials, or administrative backup.[126]

CURRENT PRACTICES IN EL PASO

Unlike the neighboring states of California and Arizona, Texas, particularly El Paso, is largely pro-bilingual. School districts espouse bilingualism in theory, finding it more valuable than moving students into English instruction as soon as possible. A large El Paso school district offers a brochure in Spanish and English illustrating its commitment to the maintenance of two languages.[127] It advertises academic excellence in two languages, high self-esteem, and multicultural understanding. The district endorses the students' native language, culture, and knowledge as the foundation for academic and social growth. Administrative support for bilingual programs and teachers trying to practice these ideals is sometimes lacking, though, when students are pushed into English-only learning environments as early as possible or when these programs are poorly funded. While the number of dual language classes is growing, they still remain very small.

Another large El Paso school district advertises its mission on let-

---

126. See Guadalupe Valdés, "The World Outside and Inside Schools: Langauge and Immigrant Children," *Educational Researcher* 27, no. 6 (1998): 4–18.

127. El Paso Independent School District. *Curriculum and Instruction, Bilingual Education* (El Paso: El Paso Independent School District, n.d.).

terhead and educators' business cards, in stating that they prepare students to be fully fluent in two or more languages and ready for higher education. While funding and other resources are not always abundant in these two districts, administrators and teachers are supportive of bilingualism, and they have had some success with their bilingual programs.

Currently bilingual education policy in El Paso is mixed, some transitional, some maintenance, some enrichment. Many view bilingual capability as a blessing. At El Paso's February 2000 Education Summit, 300 business and educational leaders endorsed bilingualism in one of the three priority goals to strengthen the city's economic future.

Bilingual education can also serve as a remedial track that segregates students by language, and it can often be coupled with income level and class. As the Texas Education Agency website shows, the test scores of the students in bilingual classes are lower than those of other students, as are scores for those taking the Spanish version of the state standardized test.[128] For this reason, El Paso ESL programs often have been looked on as remedial programs.

Some two-way dual language programs are successful in El Paso schools. In the language programs, both English-only and Spanish-only speakers are combined to create bilingual students who can function realistically at the border. Two-way programs are often combined with cooperative learning strategies that teach students to work together and think critically and that prepare them for leadership in multicultural, multilingual areas. Many see bilingualism as a distinct advantage for El Paso and Juárez, both isolated from other urban areas in their own countries by a large expanse of desert.

Another bilingual option for families in both El Paso and Juárez is to send their children to schools across the border for full immersion into the second language. In El Paso, families of Mexican heritage, as well as some Anglo parents, want their children to be fully bilingual. While their numbers are small, these parents usually send their children to private schools in Juárez to ensure fluency and rigorous aca-

128. www.tea.state.tx.us

demics. Mexican families do the same, sending their children to public and private schools in El Paso.

Most school districts in El Paso have bilingual teachers and bilingual programs for all grade levels. At the time of our research, approximately 25 percent of the Mexican American students were in bilingual programs, and about 25 percent of El Paso's teachers were bilingual. At the local university where many of the local teachers are prepared, roughly one-third of the teachers certified for elementary education are also certified as bilingual, and all teachers in training must meet a minimum Spanish-language requirement.[129]

In a second grade bilingual classroom at Schuster School, we watched a lesson on prediction and anticipation in reading, led by Ms. Guerrero, the bilingual teacher. The atmosphere was warm and friendly, and the students were chatting with Ms. Guerrero in Spanish about the books they would soon be reading. One girl had a book about a baby rattlesnake, and the teacher was asking her to look at the title, the book cover, and some of the pictures in the book to predict what the story might be about. The student, looking at the pictures of a Native American girl, guessed that the story might have something to do with the girl and what she discovered on a trail around her house. After discussing it a little further, the student wrote her prediction into her journal. Each student got to talk to the teacher or another student about what might be in his or her own book.

This prediction and anticipation lesson took place in English; the following day there would be follow up in Spanish. Here children and their teacher communicate and learn in two languages in a relaxed academic environment. Two languages are not just the norm but very natural, given the bilingual nature of the community and its families on the border.

Some bilingual teachers were Mexican immigrants themselves and started school with little or no English, yet they are fully competent in Spanish. For them, bilingual education has been successful. Others have suffered from cultural and linguistic prejudice. A bilingual teacher

---

129. Statistics from UTEP's College of Education, Teacher Education Department.

in his forties shared that as a second grader he was picked up by the teacher and placed in the class trashcan. Confused and humiliated, he later asked a friend why he had been put in the trash. The friend told him secretly in Spanish that the teacher did not allow anyone to speak Spanish in school. From then on, even after learning English, he spoke as little as possible. Lessons like these taught children (at best) that their maternal language, if not English, was something they needed to throw away. At worst, they taught children that those in authority could treat them like garbage. What we value in language and expect in classrooms have changed significantly since this incident. The child, now a teacher himself, has authority to protect students from mistreatment based on language.

Mexican American bilingual teachers often serve as cultural role models for their students. Cultural expectations of students and teachers are likely to be more similar than those between more mainstream teachers and their students. Anglo teachers, too, with cultural understanding, can be role models, showing an appreciation for differences, building on the diversity in their classes to enrich all groups.

Bilingual classrooms are places where children's language and the knowledge they learn at home are built into the curriculum, just as monolingual English classrooms build on the language and cultural knowledge Anglo children bring to school. We observed a lesson on classification in a bilingual first grade classroom at Vilas School. The whole lesson was in Spanish, directed by the bilingual teacher, Ms. Gunther. She had brought in an apple and an orange and asked the students to help her list how the two fruits were similar and how they were different. Using the concept of a Venn diagram, Ms. Gunther drew two large intersecting circles on poster paper, labeling one circle "oranges" and the other circle "apples." She labeled the middle intersecting area "oranges and apples." Students called out qualities of the fruits and where they should be listed: "red" for example, went with apples, "rough texture" with oranges, and "sweet" with both, in the middle.

After the Venn diagram lesson in Spanish, the teacher led the students in a song, in English, about fruit. The song was humorous, having students replace vowels in the words. The first line went, "I like to eat apples and bananas." In the second line, they exchanged all the regular vowels with an "eee" sound: "eee leek teee eeet eeeples eeend beeneenees." They stood at their desks singing, laughing, and moving to the rhythm of the music. Ms. Gunther put her hands on the shoulders of a little boy who was not moving to the music, and gently rocked him to the rhythm.

CURRENT PRACTICES IN JUÁREZ

In Juárez, ESL is used to enrich students for personal benefit on the border. In the early 1990s, state level administrators from the Office of Special Programs mounted a program called *Construyendo el Futuro* as part of Mexico's *modernización* program. Their objective is to give students the basic knowledge and tools to learn English and use it in daily life. This was one of the first few bilingual programs in public education on the border; recently more have been started in other border towns and a few programs exist in the interior of Mexico. Through this program, ESL classes are offered in neighborhoods to all economic levels, in both the afternoon and the morning classes.

The ESL program was first piloted in fifteen schools, grades fourth, fifth, and sixth, reaching more than 1,500 students throughout the city. ESL teachers travel from school to school spending three hours per week at each school. In theory, they use participatory methods such as Total Physical Response (TPR), a method used to involve students through experience, physical movement, and natural settings, focusing on oral comprehension and enjoyment, rather than repetition or translation. In practice, though, audio lingual ("listen and repeat") and grammar/translation methods are combined with the more engaging TPR methods. Yet, Juárez students seem to be eager to learn English, and they participate readily no matter what the method. They tell us that this is an opportunity for cross-border friendships and better economic possibilities in the future.

At Revolución School we observed several of the eight ESL classes. In the first class we visited, students were attentive (although one boy was eating a bologna sandwich). The room was decorated with several decorations, a watch-shaped clock on the wall, a map, and a colorful chart on English verbs. A wood fire burned in the shell of an old disemboweled electric heater. After a brief review of the lesson, the ESL teacher, Mr. Ochoa, dictated, "*Hay nueve lapices anaranjados.*" The students cut out five scrambled, translated words from a strip of paper and glued them into their notebooks: "There are nine orange pencils." As they cut and glued, Mr. Ochoa went around the room asking a few students to read their English sentence out loud, then the whole class repeated the sentence.

Juárez ESL classes differ in principle from El Paso ESL or bilingual classes. They do not reinforce a home language or culture that is different from the mainstream, but they teach competence in a "foreign" language, and thus reinforce their first language and cultural identity. ESL classes in Juárez are in demand in elementary school through college, but as in the United States, there are not enough trained teachers. ESL lessons, once primarily for wealthy Juarenses attending private schools in Juárez or El Paso, have now become a part of everyday classroom activity for students enrolled in the state and federal schools of Juárez.

We observed another ESL lesson at Nicolas Bravo School. The regular classroom teacher sat at her desk while Mr. Avila, the English teacher, leads the group. The class is conjugating the verb "to have": "I have, you have, she/he/it has," then using it in a sentence, "I have a yellow ribbon." Next they discuss the words to the song "Tie a Yellow Ribbon," one student asking if you tie a tie. Taking the student's lead, Mr. Avila talks about homonyms and serendipitous connections in language, "Yes, you can tie a tie, and you can tie a yellow ribbon." At this point he leads the students in singing as they read their notes to "Tie a Yellow Ribbon." When we showed the tape to Mr. Avila and the class about a month later, he noted that not all the students were singing along, and he did a quick self-critique of what he would do next time to improve the lesson. We pointed out, though, that all the students watching the video were singing along with the video, without written notes.

Photo by Susan Rippberger

English lesson, Juárez school.

In another school, Plutarco Elias Calles,[130] we observed an ESL lesson, with the English teacher, Mr. Orozco. He had grouped fourth, fifth, and sixth grade students together for a lesson on pronouns and family members, for example, "her father . . . his grandmother . . . my sister." There were forty-six students in the room, all engaged, calling out answers, waving their hands and arms to be called on to go to the board and recite parts of the lesson. Mr. Orozco had pictures representing family members lined up along the chalk tray of the blackboard. After a general introduction of family members and pronouns, students took turns pointing out the grandmother or the sister and making a sentence indicating a relationship: "She is her sister . . . he is her father."

From an evaluation by the SEP, approximately 99 percent of the children in the English program thought that the ESL classes were active and interesting and they looked forward to more. When asked why they liked the program, they first mentioned that knowing

---

130. Calles was president of Mexico during the early 1920s.

English would open work opportunities for them. Second, they said that knowing English would help them advance to *secondaria*; and third, that it would help them to be able to communicate better. Parents, too, were surveyed and most (97 percent) saw ESL as necessary and practical for the future, for self-development, and for work. Proficiency levels were also tested each year of the program and found to be quite high. Children typically scored within an 80 to 95 percent range for beginning English.

On more than one occasion, students in Juárez have approached us, using the English they had learned, to greet us: "Good morning, Miss," "How are you?" or just, "Hi!" They were always pleased that we could understand them. Some just wanted to hear us say something in English—laughing and trying to imitate us as we spoke to them in English.

We observed various types of bilingual education in Juárez, in both private and public schools, using variations of TPR in active, engaging lessons. Arriving late to a computer inauguration in winter, we found the students in formation in the main courtyard, all doing TPR commands to keep them from getting restless or cold. Students called out for different ESL teachers to take turns leading the students in commands: "Touch your head." "Turn around and jump up and down." "Touch your nose and stand on one foot."

In Juárez, English as a foreign language is the most common form of bilingual education. While English is valued as a status language in Juárez, it is unfortunate that policy planners do not show the same excitement or provide the same support for indigenous languages, showing how power shapes values, which in turn shape curriculum.

Until recently, the bilingual classrooms for Native Mexicans were only in rural indigenous areas, such as the mountains of Chihuahua for Rarámuri[131] children. Earlier, those who immigrated to Juárez were not enrolled in school. A Juárez administrator explained, "We can't enroll

---

131. *Tarahumara* is what outsiders call this community; *Rarámuri* is the name they use for themselves.

them, we have no bilingual program to meet their needs." Juárez, a city approaching 2 million people, most originally from other parts of Mexico, now has three bilingual classrooms (Rarámuri/Spanish) that serve Rarámuri children.

In El Paso, much of what counts for ESL is language structure, vocabulary, and verb forms, rather than communication skills. Students copy sentences and vocabulary lists often. The same is true in Mexico, yet the students seem to feel they are receiving a special treat, and they enjoy the lessons. When they see themselves in the video repeating semi-useless sentences, for example, "There are nine orange pencils," they happily repeat the sentence along with the video in chorus. Interestingly, El Paso teachers viewing the same video clip show disdain, saying, "Ugh, rote learning!" adding, "Kids will never learn that way." Yet in this context they do, and even enjoy learning that way. Children do not take these lessons for granted, and they can be appreciative learning a second language that they see as valuable for present and future communication needs.

CONCLUSION

At the El Paso–Juárez border, we observed a great fluidity in language programs for a region in which bilingual capability is central to the future of its economic and social development. We saw competing values in language and identity, some based on a pluralism that built on bilingualism, others that reinforce a hierarchy of languages. Bilingual teachers and administrators on both sides of the border bring a social dynamism into classrooms, where students learn much more than language. In El Paso, while we saw school brochures that promote bilingualism and biculturalism we also saw relics of the remedial approach to bilingual education that attempt to assimilate students to English, thereby reinforcing a hierarchy of languages.

In Juárez, we saw the development of an innovative language program that supports Mexican "unity" in its desire to be globally involved, along with the emergence of bilingual schools for Native

Mexican children. The once monolithic Mexican ruling party, the PRI (Partido Revolucionario Institucional[132]) promoted a mainstream national identity through its slogan "*Todos somos Mexicanos primeros.*"[133] Assimilation policies in both countries tend to marginalize those who, because of language, culture, color, or social class, do not fit into the mainstream. Teaching English in Juárez or El Paso comes within a context of language policies set by central educational administrators. Policymakers' priorities, stemming from their views of class and privilege, influence the types and methods of ESL offered and the opportunities provided for different students. At the same time, though, popular culture, administrators with a vision, and legislation can mitigate language elitism and create new paradigms for thinking about language and culture.

---

132. Institutional Revolutionary Party.

133. First and foremost we are Mexicans.

CHAPTER 6

Technology: Autonomy and Control

Asked if he used a Pentium computer, a Juárez teacher responded wryly, "No—lentium," joking about Mexico's lag in computer technology.[134]

As the teacher's response implies, technology for most people lags in Mexico, a constant reminder of the economic contrast between the two countries. Technology is significant, both symbolically and practically, to educators in the United States and Mexico. Symbolically, it represents progress, economic advantage, and power. Practically, it represents a means to jobs, information, and advanced studies, as well as a capacity for close surveillance. Technology can provide an efficient means by which accountability is established for students and teachers, but a centralized, top-down system of accountability can also disempower students and teachers. Standardized testing, for example, can provide an efficient means of comparing schools across the nation, but it prescribes teaching methods that rely more on rote learning than on thoughtful reflection and practice.

While many children of middle- and upper-income backgrounds

---

134. A pun on the word *lento*, or slow; his computers were not as fast as *Pentium* implied, but older and slower.

have computers and updated technology at home, the same is not true for children from modest economic areas. More recently, through U.S. government grants in El Paso and Special Programs in Juárez, children from underserved populations are receiving computer training in public schools. These programs, providing access to technology and training for teachers, are well received by teachers and students alike. The quality of knowledge and use of computers vary, though, in both Mexico and the United States. Some classrooms have Internet access to provide the skills to manipulate information and images for personal and academic projects. Others have older computers with outdated software, and teachers with very little training in computers.

This chapter examines what technology means for students, teachers, and administrators in El Paso and Juárez, and the connections between technology in education and the underlying issues of civics and nationality. Nationally, technology is a symbol of economic advantage and worldwide assimilation to the English language and U.S. culture since much of the software is in English. The importance of computers in both countries is symbolically very high for both national development and individual achievement.

In the United States, technology, as both mainstream and cutting edge in everyday life, is also part of the culture of accountability, surveillance, and rapid grading of standardized testing. On another level, it can mean greater autonomy in learning for students who can do research using the Internet, communicate with friends via e-mail, and collaborate on computer-based learning projects. It also has the potential to change traditional student–teacher relationships and the learning atmosphere when students coach their teachers on computer use.

BORDER SCHOOLS AND TECHNOLOGY

In public schools at the border, clear differences exist in the amount of resources dedicated to technology in public schools. The contrast ranges from state-of-the art equipment worth millions of dollars north of the border to thousands of dollars plus donations of technology south of the border. Resources on the U.S. side of the border come

from local, state, and national governments, as well as business interests, but this was more rare in Juárez. Older desktop computers, printers, mostly English software, and an occasional VCR are now common
in Juárez public schools. In El Paso, public school technology can
include lap- and desk-top computers, scanners, CD players, video
equipment (cameras, VCRs, editing machines), digital still cameras,
access to the Internet, and video conferencing. The global reach of
computers holds the promise of speedy interaction across borders, but
with that promise unrealized as yet, the current situtation highlights
national discrepancies.

Entering a computer lab in a Juárez school, we noticed two students per computer. The students stood up and greeted us formally as
we crossed the threshold. We walked around the lab, observing and
chatting with the students, and then we stopped to work with a student on the computer. Without being asked, students from across the
lab passed us the only mouse pad in the room. The lab had twenty-five
computers, sitting on tabletops side by side, three-fourths of which
were in good working condition, one printer and no Internet connection. The room was not airtight, so heat, cold, and dust carried by
desert winds sift in easily. Students are bused from other schools once
per week to learn computer skills in the ten schools throughout the
city. They learn basic computer skills, word processing, and a variety of
educational programs, one of which is a program created by the SEP on
Mexico's resources and geographical history. Teachers and administrators are very proud of this Spanish language software made nationally.

Labs in El Paso schools were somewhat different. There is often
one lab per school, most are equipped with accessories, and they are
connected to the Internet. In addition, individual classrooms usually
have several computers and printers. The Internet connection is very
important to teachers, who describe it as "integral," and "immediate" in
their daily lessons. One sixth grade teacher explained why:

> The important thing is to have more time in computer labs or more
> computers in the classroom . . . I think we should have Internet access
> in both locations because you can do considerably more integration of

computer technology into the curriculum if both are available to the students.

Computers and technology are increasingly becoming part of the learning process in El Paso schools. In Juárez the "technification" process has begun, too, but it has not reached public elementary schools to the same degree.

JUÁREZ COMPUTER PROGRAMS

The largest public university in Juárez has government-funded state-of-the-art computer equipment, with distance learning labs that equal institutions in El Paso. For public elementary and secondary schooling, though, computer equipment is usually donated by international businesses in Juárez and El Paso.

Computer donations can represent both patronizing and genuine goodwill in a border situation in which the two nations are not on an equal par economically. El Paso service clubs, businesses, and private schools have donated outdated computer equipment to schools in Juárez that otherwise would have no computers or other technology. Donated equipment, which sometimes works and sometimes does not, is transformed into working labs through an agreement with the SEP and the Universidad Autónoma de Ciudad Juárez[135] (UACJ) Computer Science Department. Through a program devised by SEP administrators in the program, *Construyendo el Futuro*, graduating students in computer science programs do their required hours of *Servicio Social*[136] by cleaning, repairing, and piecing together computer parts to create whole labs for students. This "Frankenstein" composite computer project, as one SEP official calls it, serves as a practical demonstration of their university training as well as an opportunity for them to take part in community development.

Most of the software, also donated, is in English. One exception is

135. Autonomous University of Juárez City.

136. Social Service; required internship or service in their field of study.

the SEP-created computer program in Spanish, *Mi México*, about Mexico's natural resources. Teachers and students find this program much more useful, and they welcome the opportunity to learn the geography, history, and demographics of their country, from a Mexican perspective and in their students' first language.

As researchers, we were invited to attend and support each of the computer lab inaugurations. These events were always formal community-wide celebrations that built on binational collaboration of the schools, the SEP, UACJ, UTEP, and local businesses. The first donation of thirty computers for a lab came from a Japanese-owned *maquiladora* in Juárez.

Computer lab inaugurations in Juárez and the surrounding towns were always a grand ceremony and celebration to mark this step forward in the local history of Juárez education and El Paso–Juárez collaboration and collegiality. At one inauguration, the school director and president of the parent committee greeted us and led us to the inner courtyard for the ceremony. Our walkway was lined with uniformed students who greeted us. As we filed by, a student pinned a name tag on each of us that was decorated with a tiny Mexican flag and a striped *sarape*.[137] We were then ushered to a long table on a platform in the central courtyard. Here we sat with the governor of Chihuahua, the rector of the UACJ, the director of the elementary school, the president of the parent committee, a representative from the state SEP office, and a representative of the U.S. service club that donated the computers. In the courtyard, uniformed students stood at attention by class with their teachers. In attendance also were parents, community members, the governor's engagement planners and bodyguards, and the local press and television reporters, indicating the importance of the event.

Once everyone was in place, the ceremony started with *Honores a la Bandera*, complete with a color guard and bugle corps in full black wool military uniform (long belted coat, and skirts and knee-high boots for girls, and long pants and black shoes for boys) even though the temperature was in the upper nineties. Everyone stood at attention

---

137. A blanket.

Mi México, *computer program in Spanish,* hecho en México.

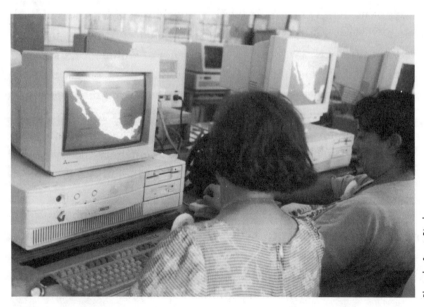

Teachers in computer lab, Juárez school.

CENTRO DE COMPUTO
"Construyendo el Futuro"

INAUGURACION

Computer lab inauguration program.

to say the flag salute, sing the national anthem, and watch as the color guard marched out, to the bugle corps. The director of the school then introduced each guest, who stood and nodded to the students and others in attendance.

The director delivered a special welcome speech, followed by a student who welcomed us, saying how honored the school was to have us with them participating in this "cultural exchange." She described how this technology project would help "pioneer" their way on the Internet and would enhance learning and cooperation for all of us. Following the student's welcome, the governor spoke to the group, first thanking the computer donors, then addressing the students, teachers, and parents on the importance of technology in education.

The governor then gave an impromptu speech to the students affirming the importance of computer literacy. Taking a portable microphone and leaving the stage of invited guests, he approached the students standing in rows. He asked them to come closer several times until they formed a close circle around him. His style was personal, directing all his attention to the students and their interests. Speaking informally about the importance of computers in their future, he made eye contact, putting his hand on boys' shoulders, touching a girl's cheek affectionately as he talked. He asked the students how many had worked on computers and what they thought of them, drawing an analogy between computers and cars; how in earlier days, people didn't need to drive but that now cars and driving are a part of life. In the same way, he explained the necessity of computers for these students. The students listened carefully and respectfully, and they seemed quite impressed.

At the end of his talk, the governor promised to continue to support education and technology. During an election year on the border, his message showcased the value of technology for the future of Mexico, a neighbor of the United States, within a government framework of *Modernization*. It also showed his commitment to students and cross-cultural exchanges, symbolically, at least. Unfortunately funding remains very low and computer labs sadly under equipped in Juárez public schools.

A ribbon-cutting ceremony followed the speeches. The director led the governor and other guests to the new computer lab door that had been adorned with a large green ribbon. An older schoolgirl held a tray with scissors that the governor used to cut the ribbon, allowing guests in to view the new computer center.

At each inauguration, refreshments followed the tour of the lab during which the participants expressed mutual appreciation for the work that had gone into the computer lab and into making it a successful part of the curriculum. It was also a time to cement friendships and partnerships in our binational effort. At other computer inaugurations, the school directors planned lunches, dances, and festivities for those in attendance, bringing out the community and, sometimes, visiting mayors from nearby towns. We found that Juárez communities valued a public affirmation of these progressive steps in education, especially since computer labs are not part of the basic public school package provided by the government.

While computer labs continue to be organized, and students and teachers rejoice in their realization, there were political agendas played out behind the scenes. These political struggles reveal some of the inner workings (or unravelings) of civics and politics in education. We witnessed some of the difficulties of donating and transporting computers, and some of the license schools take when they want to include computers and technology in their programs. School administrators frequently experienced difficulty getting donated computers across the border. Border officials, representing another arm of the government, often refused to allow their entrance even though administrators had signed documentation from the SEP office at the state capital.

In a highly centralized educational system, we were surprised at the initiative individual school directors could take in adjusting school programs for specific opportunities. Directors often suspended classes for special events. For each of the computer inaugurations, students came to school, but classes were suspended as teachers and administrators prepared for the opening ceremony. On one occasion, in which a team from UTEP was to give an in-service on the Internet and help provide the know-how and equipment to link the school to the Internet, the school director suspended school for the day. She then

Photo by Susan Rippberger

Computer inauguration celebration, Chihuahua.

invited about fifty students and twenty computer teachers from schools
in the area to take part. We had planned to help them set up their first
Internet connection and start the students writing to El Paso students
via e-mail. The El Paso classrooms were standing by to receive our first
few messages and respond—to give the students the flavor of immediate long-distance communication.

We introduced the concept of the Internet, what it is, how to get
connected, and what you can do with it once connected. Unfortunately
when we went to hook up, computers were not compatible with the
modem, among other equipment mismatches and no service provider,
so the connection was not made while we were there. That day we
chatted with the teachers over a huge meal prepared by the parent
committee, and an article appeared in the local newspaper about our
working on a project to reinforce learning and promote cultural
exchanges with students in the United States through an Internet pilot
program starting at that school.[138]

138. Heraldo de Chihuahua, "Se Integra a Internet la Escuela Porfirio Parra," *El Heraldo
de Chihuahua,* December 11, 1996.

Computer lab, Chihuahua, Mexico.

Computer lab, Chihuahua, Mexico.

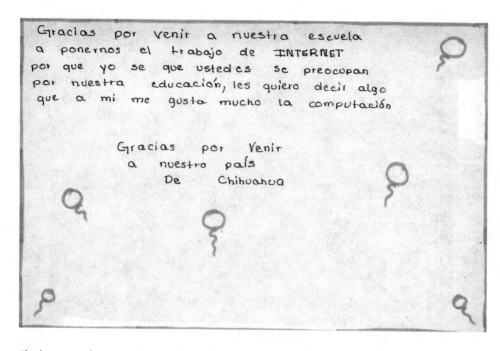

Thank-you note from a computer student, Chihuahua: "Thank you for coming to our school to set up the Internet, and because I know you care about our education I want to tell you something, I like computers very much. Thank you for coming to our country, Chihuahua."

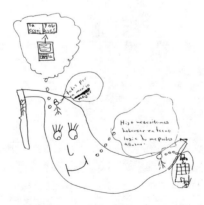

Picture drawn by Juárez student. The student is saying, "Everyone for a better Mexico." The map of Mexico replies to the student, "Son, we need to advance in technology, you can help me," The student writes to the researchers, "Thank you for coming." On the computer screen at the top, the words say, "the economy" and "obey the law."

EL PASO COMPUTER PROGRAMS

Technology in the United States is changing the way we look at education: from the way we teach students to what we teach to classroom relationships. It is affecting the way teachers organize their day, their lessons, and the way children see themselves as learners. From this perspective, computers can help to break down hierarchical relationships in schools.

In the El Paso area we found that most primary classrooms are equipped with at least one computer; some have many and the use of computers varied with teachers' training, know-how, and creativity. In some cases, computers sit unused and/or in disrepair; in others, computers are used as word processors only; in others, computers are used to enrich and enhance lessons with students exploring Internet sources for data and graphics in creating their own reports.

In a fifth grade El Paso classroom that we observed, the teacher had set up computer research stations, one that used a CD-ROM encyclopedia on geography and another that was connected to the Internet with websites already identified. A student told us what she liked about computers,

> I like using the Internet more than researching from a book . . . it has
> neat stuff like graphics and pictures that we can download and put in
> our research project. And there are so many websites that we can use.

Computer labs in El Paso usually have about twenty computers, one student per computer, with several black-and-white printers. Some labs have color printers and scanners. Here students work on their individual research projects under the guidance of the lab instructor. Much of the computer equipment and software we viewed was funded by a U.S. Department of Education grant[139] that focused on technology for low-income urban schools.[140] Teachers involved earn a master's

---

139. 1995 Technology Innovation Challenge Grant to UTEP.

140. Susan Rippberger directed UTEP doctoral students Isabel Vallejo, Timothy Quezada, Terry-Ann Rodríguez and master's degree student Allison Ring in conducting the qualitative evaluation for this grant. The evaluation team visited grant schools weekly to observe and interview students and teachers individually and in focus groups.

degree in educational technology, learning how to use computers, troubleshoot computer problems, and, most important, integrate technology into their everyday classroom lessons and activities.

Students, their parents, and their teachers found computer and technology training to be valuable for engaged learning. One of the significant elements of the technology project was to involve teachers in a master's degree program on educational technology so they could mentor other teachers at their schools. A teacher involved in the grant emphasized the importance of technical training:

> It was not until I got into the grant that I started learning how to use some of the authoring tools . . . like Digital Chisel, Hyperstudio, that I was able to finally say, "Oh! Now I know what I can do with the kids in the classroom with multimedia."

Another told us about the program:

> What the grant is doing is giving teachers an opportunity to go back to school to learn about technology . . . not offered before. The more teachers you get involved the more it spreads across the school because other teachers see what you are doing so they want to be a part, too. Of course in the long run it's the children who benefit.

A new culture of technology and learning seems to be emerging in the classrooms, where technology is not a sideline but integrated with other learning activities—thinking, creating, writing, and disseminating knowledge. As teachers and students understood technology better, they wanted greater access, and they were willing to write grants themselves for more equipment and training.

In a fourth grade bilingual classroom we visited, students were involved in a mentoring project with first grade students from another class. First graders had constructed a storyboard in their home classroom with pages that would be reproduced with Hyperstudio software as separate cards and stacks (means for organizing information electronically). The multimedia cards contained graphic artwork with accompanying narratives that explained the story line. An audio recording of each student telling her or his story was included as a button on the Hyperstudio card. Each fourth grader helped a first grader to integrate text, graphics, and audio recordings into their stories.

In another fourth grade classroom a student told us, "We are creating our own webpage, we contact people around the world through the Internet, plus we search for webpages by other students." Her friend added, "We go in to do research on the Internet almost everyday in our class—you go into the webpage site, and make a link or you can just take graphics and pictures out of it for class." Here, students are engaged more in their learning, making decisions on what they want to learn and how to go about getting the information they need. They collaborate with other students, work through problems, and do not worry about remembering facts.

We observed that teachers were asking students to help them with computer problems. Here we noticed the locus of expertise change from teacher to student, redefining their relationship. Teachers also explained to us how roles change in the teacher-student relationship. Students with more expertise than their teachers show classmates and teachers new ways to perform tasks on the computer. A teacher told us:

> Success is when they teach me something. Because they can come in
> and show me something I've been trying to figure out—and they can
> help me. They're being the teacher and I think that's cool, and they do
> too.

Another teacher shared with us how one of her bilingual students transcended a language barrier for a computer project. Oscar, who was about to make the transfer from Spanish to English instruction, became involved in an Internet project that he decided to present in Spanish and English. The teacher explains:

> I really liked the way Oscar presented [his project] in English to the
> principal and school adults. Then his mother came and some other
> people and he presented it in Spanish—he translated it. My principal
> made a point to tell me how she had noticed a change in him, that he
> was more confident. . . . that was very pleasing to me because it
> showed that even with limited English proficiency, student technol-

ogy opens doors and allows for more experiences utilizing the
English language.

Some of the effects of technology, though, are not so progressive.
Computer technology can also reinforce top-down control over
schools, channeling students' civic education into a multiple-choice
test format, where rote learning is valued over experiential learning.

TECHNOLOGY AS ACCOUNTABILITY AND CONTROL

In El Paso and Juárez, student achievement is represented by grades
and year-end exams. El Paso students are also subjected to independent achievement tests to determine what students ought to
know at a particular grade level. In the last two decades, test-based
accountability has been used to document students' performance on
what can be measured. Even though systems of testing/accountabil-
ity may have been established to compare educational programs,
affirming privilege for those with higher scores, it has become a
means to make sure that those students and regions with lower scores
are not ignored.

Preparing students whose first language is not English for an
English standardized test can be problematic, not just in El Paso. This
is a growing problem since the numbers of students for whom English
is not their dominant language has tripled in the United States since
the 1980s. In some states, schools do not have to count the non-
English speakers in the passing rates for these tests, although in Texas
they have done so since the mid-1900s. Students, principals, and
teachers are highly motivated to perform well on the tests.

States deal with the legislated demand for standardized testing in
different ways. California is legally challenging test requirements that
all students be tested in English. New York tests students in Spanish,
Russian, Chinese, Korean, and Haitian Creole. In Massachusetts
teacher organizations and others are calling for a boycott of standardized testing. Texas, often showcased because of its standard bilingual
and dual language programs, tests in Spanish. Texas goes to great

efforts to see that schools raise the scores of all students, regardless of race or ethnicity.

For administrators and teachers who work with low-income students and students of color, accountability systems require that they provide students at least a minimal amount of education. Since the report *A Nation at Risk* in 1983, public concerns over school standards have prompted policymakers to install a series of performance-based expectations for each grade level. While these provide clarity and increased rigor for school administrators, teachers, and students, they can also be chameleon-like, with changing definitions of high, mediocre, and low standards. Unfortunately, the standards that are assessed often ask students to practice lower-order thinking skills, involving memorizing particles of unconnected information that is soon forgotten. Rarely do standardized tests ask for higher-order thinking skills that involve deep analysis or evaluation. Rarely do they expect the test takers to express themselves orally or in writing, or to put their knowledge into practice for the benefit of their community. Skills such as these are not as easily quantified for quick comparison.

Teachers use software packages to provide practice for the standardized year-end testing, although these were not the most popular uses of technology. A third grade teacher told us how she integrated Internet information with the Texas Assessment of Academic Skills (TAAS) practice:

> *Weekly Reader* and *Time for Kids* have archives with a lot of information, so I pull that down from the Internet and print it up. Then we read them in the classroom because they're short, fact-filled pieces of information which are ideal for practicing the TAAS: fact, opinion, finding information, looking for details, so that's very good for me.

Achievement can be measured in many ways: multiple-choice questions, short answers, open-ended questions, long essay responses, science projects, research papers, and portfolios, each measuring different types of learning. Those measures that are easiest to score and compare are not the most relevant for measuring achievement, but they seem to have an appeal for policymakers. The value placed on numer-

ical comparisons shows both a simplistic view of learning and a pro-
clivity for labeling and affirming those in the mainstream who typically
do well on these types of tests.

In the United States, and in Texas specifically, teachers, principals,
and superintendents are judged publicly on classroom, campus, and
district scores. Superintendents and teachers are publicly praised for
raising scores, whether it is because students actually learn more or
because they have more resources for test preparation programs. The
technological tools that allow policymakers and the wider public to
judge teachers' and students' performance are not yet in place in Juárez,
for better or worse, so top-down control is more diffused.

Some El Paso schools and classrooms are even given cash rewards
for raising scores. For those who do not raise scores, their "failure" is
also made public knowledge, sometimes in an article in the local newspaper. Because testing is often a caricature of practical knowledge that
does not even touch on a love for learning or growth in understanding
a topic, an obsession with testing can be injurious to learning. Rather
than holding students accountable for civic knowledge, skills, and predispositions, for example, students are asked "objective,"that is testable
questions in machine-gradable formats. Technology is used to track,
sort, and reward or penalize students in high-stakes accountability systems, undermining, rather than facilitating, broad civic education.
However, at the same time it brings attention to areas and populations
that have been neglected economically for years, and it makes district
officials, administrators, and teachers responsible for student failure,
even if in meaningless ways.

ACCOUNTABILITY AND CIVICS

In both Juárez and El Paso, educational modernization goes hand in
hand with independent measures of achievement. The case for national
standards has been a bipartisan effort in the United States, rising during
the late 1980s Republican administration, and continuing through the
1990s Democratic administration. Debates persist over such issues as
whether testing should be voluntary or compulsory, where funding

Juárez students taking an exam in the computer lab.

should come from, and whether all students should be tested or just a sampling. Advocates for national standards use the dismal results of U.S. students at middle and high school levels, compared to their counterparts in European and Asian countries, to argue for national standards tests. The InterAmerican Development Bank plots Mexico's math performance as average in the Americas, south of the United States.[141]

As teachers and school districts are held more accountable via standardized testing, preparation for tests tends to subvert experience-based learning. We observed in El Paso schools that in some cases, lessons are based more on paper and pencil drills for the test than

---

141. On the standards movement, see Diane Ravitch, *National Standards in American Education.* (Washington, D.C.: Brookings Institution Press, 1995). Also see annual *Brookings Papers on Educational Policy.* On questions about standardized testing, see Susan Ohanian, *One Size Fits Few: The Folly of Educational Standards* (Westport, Conn.: Heinemann, 1999), Alfie Kohn, *The Case against Standardized Testing: Raising the Scores, Ruining the Schools* (New York: Heinemann, 2000), chap. 3, many issues of *Rethinking Schools* (www.rethinkingschools.edu), and the Fair Test website (*www.fairtest.org*). On the InterAmerican Development Bank, see Paul Constance, "A Call to Action in the Classroom" *IDBAMERICA* (March–April, 1999): 22–23.

participatory learning activities. The *Washington Post*, reporting on the pervasiveness of testing, quotes a sixth grader who has been influenced by the testing ideology of his school, "If we fail, we're doomed. If we pass, we're cool."[142] Other students, less influenced by testing norms, see failing or sabotaging the tests as "cool."

TECHNOLOGY AND CIVICS IN JUÁREZ

Although Juárez has computers for student use, it is not yet using technology to document what students have learned through standardized tests and achievement scores. Mexico has year-end exams for each subject and grade level. These teacher-graded tests, along with the teachers' evaluations (including their students' attendance, effort, and ability) determine whether students advance to the next grade level. Juárez does not reveal these scores publicly for comparison by classrooms, campus, or region like El Paso. Traditionally, the government has been discreet, even secretive, releasing reports and budgets very carefully. Yet the Mexican government has embraced Internet openness with complicated, even dazzling websites for its cabinet-level departments and institutes. Still, the amount of information they install online is more limited than, for example, the Texas Education Agency or the U.S. Department of Education.

From the SEP's website, we obtained guidelines for civic knowledge, and expectations for students' learning in the first year of *secundaria*.[143] What students are expected to learn includes: (1) laws, that is, fundamental rights and responsibilities, (2) the rights of children and youth, (3) the right to education (including democracy, equality, liberty, justice, and fraternity, and knowledge about the SEP), (4) rights and responsibilities for a healthy life, (5) the right to personal security, (6) the right to free time (culture and sports), (7) the right to work, (8) lib-

---

142. Phillip Pan, "For Some New to U.S. Schools, English Itself Is Biggest Test," *Washington Post*, September 7, 1999.

143. roughly equivalent to seventh grade in the United States.

erties, and (9) equality of rights and obligations in the struggle against discrimination. These expectations for learning embody a rights-oriented focus, including knowledge about education. The rule of law is a basic foundation to enforce rights, in theory at least, since the independence of Mexico's judiciary is not as strong as in many other democracies.

For the second year of *secundaria*, SEP goals for civics include the following: (1) how the nation is organized, (2) Mexico as a republic, (3) division of powers, (4) the municipality (local government), (4) democracy and representation, (5) the vote, elections, and political parties, (6) the nation (symbols of nationality, such as the flag and the national anthem), and (7) national sovereignty (placing Mexico in a regional and global context in which sovereignty, self-determination, and nonintervention are highly valued). Studies emphasize the importance of government, situating Mexico in regional and global contexts. The international focus is not found in Texas/U.S. priorities. This would stand to reason since the United States, as an independent nation, has not been invaded by any other country, so national sovereignty would be less an issue than is a concept like Manifest Destiny.

TECHNOLOGY AND CIVICS IN EL PASO

Technology to document what students learn flourishes in El Paso. It is difficult to devise and score a testing instrument for the over 50 million children in the U.S. school population from diverse backgrounds. Test concepts and items are politicized. Science, for example, is a content area as well as a process of inquiry—not easy to reduce to test questions. Civic education, like science, is an activity as well as a topic, which, when subjected to testing, can either enhance or undermine civic education.

Examples from the voluntary National Assessment of Educational Progress (NAEP) and state civics tests show the types of knowledge students in El Paso are asked to learn. El Paso takes its lead from TAAS and the Texas Essential Knowledge and Skills (TEKS) standards.

The National Assessment of Educational Progress (NAEP) test for civics is administered every decade for a sample of approximately 30,000 public and private school students at the fourth, eighth, and twelfth grade levels. Questions reflect three levels, *basic*, *advanced*, and *proficient* standards for each grade. NAEP is made up of 60 percent multiple-choice questions and 40 percent short-answer questions. Examples that follow show the complexity of the knowledge students are expected to master in eighth grade, on two of the three levels (basic and advanced).

(A) basic level example:

As a whole, the Bill of Rights mostly addresses the rights of
  a. states
  b. individuals
  c. cities
  d. public officials

(B) advanced level example:

When two [people] come into [the Supreme] Court, one may say: "an act of Congress means this." The other may say it means the opposite. We [the Court] then say it means one of the two or something else in between. In that way we are making the law, aren't we?" (Earl Warren, Chief Justice of the Supreme Court)

Some people are troubled by the role of the Court described by Chief Justice Warren. Which argument could they effectively use against it?

  a. It is dangerous to give nonelected officials such as judges so much power in the government.
  b. The Supreme Court makes it too difficult for the federal government to exercise its power over the states.
  c. Supreme Court judges are the members of society most capable of making decisions about social policy.
  d. The main task of the Supreme Court is to rewrite the Constitution to respond to modern problems.

The questions in this section would be particularly difficult for students whose fifth through eighth grade textbooks contained little detail on the structure and function of cabinet departments, or for students who do not read the newspaper. The NAEP questions, administered only in English, are confusing even for native English speakers. Questions offer even more challenges to students for whom English is not the first language.

In 1998, the NAEP[144] reported that a third of students scored below basic, and only a fifth, at the advanced and proficient levels. White students achieved the highest scores, and Latinos and economically marginalized students scored the lowest. Low Latino performance on these tests may also reflect poor reading ability in a second language, English.

The Texas Assessment of Academic Skills (TAAS) for El Paso students begins in third grade, but practice for the tests begins much earlier. Teachers often call the practice tests in the earlier grades "baby TAAS." Students gear up for the tests with test-taking workshops, after-school review sessions, summer tutorials, and other supports. Ideally, these tests indicate what students know about school subjects, not how well they can take a test. Students take "mock" TAAS tests in the fall so that those at risk of failing the test get after-school tutoring. Students think about TAAS in other content areas. The following is an essay written by a student preparing for his first TAAS test:

> I think I know how to pass the Taas [sic] test. I hope I pass the Taas test. I hope I get a 4 [writing score] on the test. I hope I get a medal. In the future I hope I pass. I think I know how to pass the Taas test. I hope I pass the Taas test. I will listen all year around. I will take my time.

The student writes in whole sentences and spells almost every word correctly. However, the substance of his essay lacks significance for all

---

144. NAEP, *1998 Civics Report Card*, 1999.

but TAAS preparation. The next fall, the same student wrote, "I kept my promise to pass the TAAS test. This year I will master everything on the TAAS! I can't wait to master the TAAS. GOOD BYE!" Here an elementary school student has bought into the importance of the test, outside of any learning context. One can sense the student's exasperation ("GOOD BYE!") to bring closure to the test.

Sample TAAS questions are available to teachers to help them prepare students for the eighth grade social studies test, administered in a battery of tests on a single day each April. The Texas Essential Knowledge and Skills (TEKS), which serve as grade-level standards, are merged with TAAS questions. Teachers are expected to incorporate TEKS into their lessons as well.

The introduction to the civics section of the Texas Essential Knowledge and Skills (TEKS) lays a foundation for eighth grade civics classes, where students are expected to learn patriotism, function in a free enterprise society, and appreciate the basic democratic values of our state and nation (referenced in the Texas Education Code). It is only in eighth grade that the TAAS test covers social studies, showing that social studies is not valued as highly as math and English, which are covered more frequently.

On the TEKS list of knowledge expectations, there are nine listed for history. One of the TEKS states, "The student understands traditional historical points of reference in U.S. history through 1877." Another states, "The student is expected to explain the significance of the following dates: 1607, 1776, 1787, 1803, and 1861–1865," implying that there can be only one right event to remember about each date. Here again, the test item is presented without a context of the multiple global events that were interacting and influencing each other socially, philosophically, or politically. There are three "essential skills" listed for geography; three for economics; four for government; four for citizenship; four for culture; two for science, technology, and society; and three for social studies. Besides memorizing fact particles, students are expected to think about concepts. One TEKs, for example, is to "evaluate the contributions of the Founding Fathers [always capital-ized] as models of civic virtue." The Founding Fathers (no mention of Founding Mothers here) are largely idealized versions of the real personalities. Concepts such as who decides what skills are essential, and why they are essential, are not included in the Texas Essential Knowledge and Skills.

Educators align the TEKS with TAAS preparation, focusing on some topics more than others. Out of twenty-three general areas, the five top categories of alignment, listed in order, are: Texas Statehood, Economics, the Civil War, the Westward Expansion, and the Constitution, thus indicating the priorities of those who created the TEKS and TAAS. They highlight the structure of state and national governments, economics, and war. Other themes such as social history, the environment, and education do not receive the same status.

There are also questions on multiculturalism, evidence that this theme has been institutionalized in the curricula and tests. One of these questions asks the name of the first African American woman graduate in U.S. higher education. While this woman's entrance into higher education is a significant milestone in the history of undoing U.S. apartheid, it can also be seen as trivializing multicultural education since it isolates the event from the wider framework of a sustained struggle for justice for both African Americans and women. Here the test values what children can memorize over their understanding of the significance of the struggle that took place to allow African Americans and women equal opportunity in education, among other basic rights.

SERVICE LEARNING

Service learning, while not reducible to numerical evaluation through multiple-choice testing, is a concept that has generated some excitement among teachers in Texas. The Texas Education Agency (TEA) makes small grants available to classrooms and campuses. Teachers receive in-service training to coach students to come up with creative ideas for drafting proposals. One such idea was to make a video of the

Constitution and its amendments. A group of students created and performed one of the constitutional amendments. Learning this way, students do not forget information as they might if they had memorized it. The students' audience was made up of peers, teachers, and younger students. Only "Gifted and Talented"[145] teachers and students participated in this activity, not the majority of students. No doubt, enjoying an activity such as this helped gifted and talented students score better on the Constitution questions of the TAAS (although the project was scheduled for after the TAAS, when the school atmosphere is less tense).

In our perusal of over 200 sample TAAS questions provided for teachers, we noted that only one dealt with service learning.

> Students at your school have adopted two miles of Texas highway.
> Once a month, students gather in groups and go out to pick up trash
> and collect cans and bottles to recycle. The main benefit to the com-
> munity resulting from the service of this group of students is that:
>
>   a. The students make money by recycling the cans and
>   bottles.
>   b. The students get to spend time with friends.
>   c. People can throw trash on the highway without worrying.
>   d. The students are helping to keep the environment safe
>   and clean for everyone to enjoy.

Several of the answers can be justified here; for example, if answer "b" creates civic solidarity and a sense of belonging in students, it may be even more valuable than keeping a specific environment safe and

---

145. About 5 percent of the El Paso student population is selected for Gifted and Talented programs. Students are selected on the basis of high achievement and teacher recommendation. See Jeannie Oakes. *Keeping Track: How Schools Structure Inequality* (New Haven, Conn.: Yale University Press, 1985), on the different learning experiences school tracking systems create for students. See Edgar Litt, "Civic Education, Community Norms, and Political Indoctrination," *American Journal of Sociology* 28 (February 1963): 69–75, research on political socialization based on economic class, documenting contrasting approaches to civic education: obedience versus engagement.

clean. The choice of "a" is probably the most realistic answer given our penchant for rewards and punishment, namely, grades, pay, promotions, which will really train our children to care for the environment. But the one "correct" answer is most likely "d." This type of test values remembering a correct answer over thinking creatively or critically, and it thus reinforces conformity.

CONCLUSION

Technology in education on the border is a study in contrasts. Technology can enable students to direct their own learning and construct their own knowledge, it can be a means of control, or it can be both at the same time. It can also expose a disparity between funded and unfunded technology programs, with some receiving new equipment and software, and others receiving hand-me-downs.

Technology offers the possibility for a new culture—a community of learners, where students and teachers work more collaboratively, with more progressive, interactive teaching techniques. We see evidence of student-centered, teacher-facilitated (rather than teacher-dictated) activities. Interaction and relationships between and among students and teachers show more collegiality and openness.

Technological tools provide high-security, high-speed scoring to determine whether accountability goals are met. But the goals and assessments may result in more control over students and classrooms than necessary. Technology and accountability systems that can sort and score millions of students' work do not encourage authentic learning and self-realization. Accountability tests for social studies currently in place in Texas do not facilitate real civic learning or critical thinking and action skills that predispose students to participate in community and public affairs. Without social exercise of these skills and the knowledge underlying them, students forget details quickly; rather, they learn to conform and look for single right answers.

Individual accountability is not the same on both sides of the border. In Juárez schools students are asked to be responsible for their work, but students are rarely singled out. Teachers are also asked to be responsible for teaching well, but they are not held responsible for student failure. At a binational conference on education and ethnography in Juárez, the concept of accountability came up. The conversation first focused on translating the word itself, *accountability*. The group came up with several synonyms, like responsibility, liability, answerability. But translating the concept and its nuances of meaning and behavior was much more elusive, illustrating a difference in cultural values. While systems of accountability and technological tools expose teachers and students to new forms of surveillance, judging their performance on the basis of tests that teachers have little hand in designing, they can also open up learning beyond the textbook, allowing students to construct knowledge with teachers.

Comparing the two cities, Juárez and El Paso, we see disparate funding in public schools, but an acknowledgment of and appreciation for computer literacy as a necessity for all children. Computers used as measures and controls will continue, but not without their flip side, autonomy. In classrooms, technology can offer a new kind of learning community in which students interact socially in new ways— with each other, with teachers, and with knowledge. Students' ability to work together and with technology will be instrumental to their individual futures and to economic development on the North American continent.

CHAPTER 7

Conclusion

Entre los individuos, como entre las naciones, el respeto al derecho ajeno es la paz.[146] (Benito Juárez, 1867, president of Mexico)

The wisdom of Mexico's loved president, Benito Juárez, and for whom Ciudad Juárez is named, captures the spirit of our book. Only by mutual respect—among ourselves and across borders—do we understand one another, and thus learn to give our children an education that builds both national and binational solidarity. Cross-cultural comparisons are not simple, particularly in a border region with such fluidly blending cultures, divided by an imaginary but inflexible political line. The mutual influences and interaction between schooling and society are complex, yet schooling is one way to support cultural and national values in training children for adulthood both in work and in social life. We find that schooling on the border serves as a microcosm of society itself, as a place where society is re-created. Schools are a place of blending: in bilingual classes with some teachers educated in Juárez, in which students live in El Paso either cross daily to attend school or criss-cross for periods of time during their life. In this binational area we find that citizenship training in schools goes beyond class curricu-

---

146. Among individuals and nations, respecting the rights of one's neighbor is peace.

lum to teacher attitudes and student expectations, and that people's identity does not fit neatly into nationalistic or cultural definitions.

Children are exposed to many kinds of civic and national education in schools through classroom management, explicit historical and political instruction (some of it stridently nationalistic), and socially interactive experiential education with hands-on or problem-solving activities. Texas offers its own state versions of values, historical stories, and flags, whereas Mexico has one nationalistic curriculum that comes from the national capital. This can be perplexing for immigrant children exposed to civic education in their homelands and later in their new country. They have learned that it is appropriate to show unquestioning respect and love for government, history, and those in authority, and, later, in the United States, they must learn new individualistic social values.

Educating this diverse group of learners in U.S. classrooms presents a worthy challenge for teachers of the twenty-first century. Our hope is that societies provide their children with the kind of civic education that will move them beyond marketplace purposes and static notions of nationality to serve and challenge the public places of community, government, and civic society. We believe students need to interact socially while gaining experience in problem solving and in critical analysis for change in democratic societies. We consider not only the U.S. future but also the future of the North American region, now with some connection through NAFTA, but perhaps connected more closely in a potential future common market. Could our two countries, together with Canada, ever consider themselves as one transnational region—a North American Union—and is this something worth developing for our children?

Most schools are blessed with teachers who care about their students. However, teachers work in systems that send contradictory messages that can stifle students' civic learning and their own ability to exercise professional autonomy. Too much of what passes for civic education is ritualistic and irrelevant to students' current and future civic and social experiences.

Students seem to memorize much about history, not understanding how all the details fit together or how they fit as individuals into the historical and national scheme. Students in introductory courses at the university often do not know basic information about history or government(s). When students confuse the Vietnam War with World War II or position the American Revolution at the time of the Civil War, we wonder about the other missing pieces of civic knowledge, not to mention basic U.S. or Texas facts, for example, what happened at the Alamo? Even worse, they may memorize the "facts" they have been taught and accept them uncritically, thereby supporting ideological agendas.

Students are taught little about the world around them. U.S. and Mexican students are taught that their country exhibits the one best way to organize politics and an economy. Right or wrong, their conclusions are rarely derived from comparative studies or deep knowledge about countries elsewhere. It is vital that students appreciate their nation in global and regional contexts since we live in a complex interdependent economy.

How can it be that U.S. students remember so little about history? They learn about the Boston Tea Party, the earliest presidents, and the branches of government from first grade on, yet they acquire little more than token knowledge when it comes to the U.S. black experience, or that of women or Latinos. In elementary school they color pictures of presidents, take connect-the-facts tests, and pledge allegiance regularly. By middle school, they have memorized dates, names of agreements, and of leaders. In Texas, the questions that drive their social studies classrooms are sometimes dauntingly detailed and complex. Perhaps they remember so little because they learn many of the facts superficially, and they can forget them after the test. Perhaps it is because the bits of information they learn are not relevant in their lives. Much of the information they are asked to memorize might be more easily accessed in encyclopedias or on the Internet.

In El Paso, students rarely learn social studies in socially interactive ways that allow them to test the ideals and principles with the actual experience of public thought and action. There are exceptions to this rule, given the interest in service learning and the innovative proj-

Photo by Kathleen Staudt

IFE poster on pluralism, Juárez school: "Pluralism is getting along respectfully and peacefully with those of different opinions and political perspectives."

ects with children voting or in classes for those labeled gifted or advanced. But too few students learn in ways that build networks of trust toward action; most do not learn in association with one another, practicing democratic interaction. Citizens need skills and predispositions to do more than earn a living successfully; they need to negotiate policy agendas, too.

In Juárez, confusion about the basic facts of Mexican history is not as likely. A national identity is cultivated and renewed continuously, mixed with cultural traditions that emerge from both local communities and officialdom. Students are exposed to a consistent portrayal of the tragic and the victorious in national history, set in regional and global contexts, and reinforced with calendars, songs, and dances in school ceremonies. National guidelines for teachers are unified and centralized, although not tested through public national (or state) accountability systems that use technology for speedy assessment results of students and teachers alike.

From primary school up, Mexican students learn about constitutions, rights, and pluralism in a political system that for more than a half century defied multiparty elections. One political party had dominated the nation until the 1980s when democratic openings allowed for the victory of other political parties to be acknowledged. Budding pluralist policies, though, did not deliver on job creation, decent wages, or sustained support for food subsidies and the trickle of benefits that went to the poor majority. The aftermath of the debt and oil crises of the early 1980s set the stage for many changes in Mexico. Migration to the north continues for political and economic reasons. Migrants, however, take with them a strong sense of national pride.

The realities of Mexico's flawed democracy and economy have made many adults cynical; nevertheless, voter turnout rates since the 1980s surpassed those in the United States. In Mexico, national identity involves more than support for its political economy or national leaders. Their support is for a wider notion of historic place in the hemisphere, and a blend of cultural practices tied to Catholicism and the Spanish language.

Many in the United States might take issue with the stridency and unity of Mexico's national identity. Would such a nationally and culturally unified vision ever have been possible or likely, given the decentralization in U.S. governance? Americanization practices in schools evoke mixed values, reinforcing individualism more than community and social interaction. U.S. civic education prepares students for the opportunity-seeking behavior that characterizes the U.S. work and consumer economy.

In Mexico there is a saying that differentiates attitudes toward work: "Here, we work to live; in the United States, they live to work." Sayings like these can oversimplify outlooks, but they can also offer insight on civic education in both countries. Juárez schools teach children to value a social, national, and cultural identity, where work, although indispensable, is incidental to the meaning of life. El Paso school programs value individual cultural characteristics that lead to competition and consumption in the workplace and economy. Here work is central to life, sometimes replacing life with a flow of "busyness."

Experiential or service learning may counteract a civic education that teaches passivity and uncritical acceptance of disconnected facts. When kids vote for candidates or for their rights, they (and their parents who accompany them) see and experience real engagement. When students solve problems together, in technological teams or *Servicio Social*, they construct their knowledge in ways that deepen its impact and persist more than when they memorize details for high-stakes testing. But these experiences sometimes come too late or are available to very few in Gifted and Talented or Advanced Placement classes in the United States. Moreover, practical experience is not elevated as a "standard" that drives educators' sense of priorities and allocates time for civic tasks in classrooms. Multiple-choice accountability tests, as now in place, are not suited for the higher order thinking and action that comes with critical thinking and problem-solving activities.

Despite these differences, civic education converges in another way in both countries. Civic education, on the whole, encourages individualist acts of civic responsibility as it encourages critical thinking in advanced education, though modestly. But in both systems, most children grow into adulthood lacking knowledge, tools, and predispositions for engagement in public affairs. They live in political systems that nurture a certain incongruence between what they learned about ideals, honesty, and trust when young and what they experience as adults. The divergence between rhetoric and reality of those in authority can be startling to young adults, resulting in cynicism and disengagement from public affairs.

Are minimal public engagement and general mistrust inevitable in advanced industrial societies, such as El Paso and Juárez? The prophets of doom regarding declining community point to the overwhelming odds that nudge us away from social capital building: TV time, decline in extended and nuclear families, and so on.[147] Those

---

147. Robert Bellah et al., *Habits of the Heart* (New York: Harper & Row, 1985); Robert Putnam et al., *Bowling Alone: The Collapse and Revival of American Community*, (New York: Simon & Schuster, 2000).

International bridge — wishing those entering the U.S. a happy trip.

Photo by Susan Rippberger

forces that push communities toward individualism are especially aggravated in the United States. In Mexico, the cultural capital of extended family, the celebration of social interaction, and local culture persist. But can this Mexican cultural capital rejuvenate U.S. communities through immigrants and through adaptation of elements from Mexican education and culture? To do so, schools need to value immigrant children's cultures and their languages, respecting them as worthy of maintenance.

Not the least of the cultural benefits brought into the United States by immigrants is language capability. Our North American future, like that of Europe, depends on capability in two or more languages. In a regional and global economy, genuine bilingual or multilingual aptitude will offer intellectual, social, and national economic assets. The marketplace seems to recognize this more quickly than educational systems. We need to reevaluate bilingual education as an instrument of enrichment for both English speakers and speakers of other languages.

SUGGESTIONS FOR MORE CIVIC ENGAGEMENT IN SCHOOLS

We offer suggestions for future civic education that may encourage community engagement and more experiences in the process of civic engagement.

- Strengthen democratic interactions in classrooms and on campuses that expand voices and address mutual problem solving. Involve students in meaningful decisionmaking. Offer opportunities for children to construct knowledge about democracy in educational policymaking in critical and active ways. Engage parents in more than popcorn or enchilada dinner sales; parents are stakeholders whose voices ought to be heard in campus, district, and state policymaking.

- De-track ESL and bilingual education into dual-language instruction that begins in elementary schools. Encourage students to interact in classrooms and on playgrounds to facilitate genuine bilingual abilities and social interaction.

- Set realistic standards in civics, based on concepts and critical thinking and acting. Elevate civic priority in accountability processes, but limit standardized testing. Use tests with multiple ways of measuring civic knowledge and skills, with less emphasis on multiple-choice grades and more on writing and hypothetical problem solving.

- Increase U.S.–Mexico exposure and interaction through student and teacher exchanges, preparing for a regional community and common market in our lifetimes. Regionalize and globalize civic education: continue to value national and state public affairs and governance, but avoid hollow patriotic rituals and myths about statehoodism and nationalism.

- Reduce the obscene inequalities in wages within communities and across national borders in North America through living wages, not just minimum wages among North American partners. Resource disparities are huge, showing how little we value people as people who happen to be citizens of different nations, yet live only miles apart. And teachers' salaries within and across borders are undervalued compared to other professionals.

• De-track social studies classes separating the gifted/advanced from the regular students to permit engaging and interesting activities for all. Democratic education is for more than a few students.[148]

• Increase funding for Mexico's schools, teachers, and technology. Per-student funding gaps between Mexico and the United States are larger than per capita income or minimum wage gaps, or other indicators of inequality.

Cultural interpretations of national identity within classrooms serve to bring children into the larger national and cultural context. Both countries can benefit from these lessons, finding a balance between order and chaos and more humanistic scheduling. Achieving balance between individual freedom and community responsibility is not necessarily for the purpose of nation building but it facilitates greater learning and a more caring educational environment, and, by so doing, it benefits and strengthens a nation. Along these lines, teachers may acknowledge a need for less external control, or conformity, perhaps questioning whom this benefits. Teachers on the U. S. side of the border may want to teach more social and political history and government, without losing sight of multicultural histories, while teachers on the Mexican side may wish to teach a more critical perspective on the same topics.

By analyzing education in both cities, we begin to understand the heritages of children of the growing Latino populations in the United States, soon to become the largest "minority" group. Growing diversity demands respect for culture, language, and different types of expectations for learning. The content and style in learning need to address cultural expectations and norms. Understanding cultural differences

---

148. Kathleen Staudt, "Democratic Education for More than the Few," in *Developing Democratic Character in the Young*, ed. Roger Soder et al. (San Francisco: Jossey-Bass, 2001).

can help teachers, administrators, and policymakers address the needs of a diverse nation to increase student learning across the board and across the nation. Cross-cultural understanding also helps dismiss the stereotyping and labeling that limit student success. Students raised in Mexican culture are not always aware of the cultural mores demanded in U.S. schools, and they are thus marginalized by expectations they are not aware of.[149]

While dominant cultures influence educational systems, it is important to acknowledge and respond to the pluralism that exists within educational settings, particularly in El Paso, where approximately 80 percent of the students are of Mexican heritage. It can only enhance students' learning to respond to, and include, their unique cultural heritage and knowledge base.

Increasingly, Mexican immigrants and their children form sizable portions of large urban areas in the United States, such as Chicago and New York. Mexico is the national origin of the largest group of immigrants in America. People of Mexican heritage bring Mexican educational experiences with them throughout the United States, where corporations and the media carve special market niches based on language and culture.

For citizens as well as immigrants, public schools are one of the most comprehensive institutions of national acculturation. The border, as an area of binational relations and fluid blending, constitutes a microcosm of relations between, and values representative of, the two nations. Rather than peripheral, it is central, providing critical insight into the processes of the mainstream elements of each country—the forefront of cultural and national values and change.

Societies place an enormous responsibility on schools, socializing youth through curricula, rituals, programs, and less visible management patterns in which national values are embedded. Public schools embrace and reinforce cultural and national values to create "good" citizens.

---

149. See Pierre Bourdieu, *Outline of a Theory of Practice*, translated by Richard Nice (Cambridge: Cambridge University Press, 1995).

Fundamentally, we grapple with the questions posed by James Banks, writer on multicultural educational in the United States:

> Is it possible for citizenship education to promote justice in a highly stratified society or does citizenship education necessarily reflect and reproduce the society in which it is embedded? Whose concept is citizenship education? To whom does the concept belong? Who constructed it? Whose interests does it serve?[150]

It is important that U.S. educators understand the new majority children and their heritages so we can serve them through education and include them in civic society. The above quotation rings true in Mexico, too, where privilege, class, color, and mainstream culture dominate school policy. Civic education is, above all, a power shared with children to strengthen democracy for all.

IMMIGRATION AND CITIZENSHIP

We include here an account of a middle school immigrant student named Daniel, who along with his family, is making the most of the American dream, combining the best of both worlds, Mexico and the United States. Daniel was born in El Paso and his family has moved back and forth across the border several times during his life. His situation doesn't fit easily into state-imposed definitions of the immigrant or migrant student.

An eighth grader, Daniel is eager for a better life in the United States. Middle school counselors confirm this, saying that immigrant students are different: they have clear values, show respect for their teachers, and are eager to succeed. English is his most difficult subject, so we spoke to him in Spanish. Daniel wants to be an engineer, and he does particularly well in math. We often hear from teachers that students from Mexico bring good math skills along with confidence, not anxiety, about their ability to succeed in math. We think U.S. math

---

150. James Banks, *Educating Citizens in a Multicultural Society* (New York: Teachers College Press, 1977).

educators might do well to learn more about math pedagogy in Mexico.

Daniel remembers his classes in Mexico and misses the respect students had for their country and for civic values. He does not see respect for the motherland/fatherland in the United States. Daniel explains that he does not miss what he called "the problem with teachers," that is, the strikes and the teacher absenteeism he saw in Mexico. His mother supports the family, and she attends evening classes at the local community college to become a nurse and learn English.

Daniel explains that his teachers at the middle school are open to questions, seem interested in his progress, and some even welcome his presence after school in classrooms where he can work on the computer or do his homework. One of his classes is a "prep center" for recent immigrants who need additional support. Some of these students are U.S. citizens with passports, but they live in Juárez. The teacher, a former immigrant herself, has created a respectful and nurturing environment for the students.

Daniel's classes involve active learning and integrate themes in different content areas. For example, they drew plans for a dream house, to scale, converting measurements and discussing different possibilities. Later they wrote an essay on their dream house. Students learn content in a language they understand (Spanish), but they gradually do more and more in English. At the very beginning, they learn "survival" English and survival skill vocabulary: how to ask for food in the cafeteria, for example.

Students also learn what is expected of them, and what rights they have in the classroom. One difference they are not always aware of is that they are expected to ask questions. In their home country, questions in upper grades might be perceived as a challenge or as an interruption of class. Here, classroom freedom might prompt them to take freedom too far, or create unnecessary interruptions. So the teacher reminds students to be respectful again.

Culture shock is one of the first concerns with which the prep teacher deals. She explains cultural differences and how to deal with them, explaining students' rights and obligations. Students learn that they are encouraged to ask questions and seek instructions when they do not understand. After students gain this sense of autonomy, though, they need to learn a sense of internal control—when to interrupt and when not to, when to chat informally with a teacher, and when not to. With external control, students might become too familiar with adults or loose respect. Teachers remind them of the boundaries of their behavior.

Daniel's school and its special programs represent a better-case scenario for new immigrants than what happens in many schools, farther from the border, where immigrants are less visible. Their very invisibility, amid the culture shock they experience in a new country, could affect educational success. Immigrants and language minority students are significant, in talent and numbers. They are, and have always been, too important to the success of our nation to be ignored or miseducated in school. Without language programs that ensure students keep up academically while they are learning English, we run the risk of maintaining high dropout rates, reduced economic opportunity, and lost human potential.

The border is a region where binational relations and values are integrated. It is central in providing critical insight into demographic change and the processes of assimilation in each country, and it is at the forefront of national change. An awareness of the interconnectedness between the two cities on many levels can help teachers in both cities to respond to their students' educational needs, creating a curriculum, teaching styles, and teacher training programs that acknowledge and appreciate U.S.–Mexico solidarity.

BIBLIOGRAPHY

Aldana Rendon, Mario A. *Política Educativa del Gobierno Mexicano.* Universidad de Guadalajara: Instituto de Estudios Sociales, 1977.

Allen, JoBeth, ed. *Class Actions: Teaching for Social Justice in Elementary and Middle School.* New York: Teachers College Press, 1999.

Alvarez, Sonia, Evelina Dagnino, and Arturo Escobar. "Introduction: The Cultural and the Political in Latin American Social Movements." In *Cultures of Politics, Politics of Culture: Re-visioning Latin American Social Movements,* edited by Sonia Alvarez, Evalina Dagnino, and Arturo Escobar. Boulder, Colo.: Westview, 1998.

Anderson, Benedict. *Imagined Communities.* London: Verso, 1991.

Anderson, John Ward. "Politicians without Borders: Mexico's Candidates Court Support for Migrants in U.S." *Washington Post,* May 9, 2000, A20.

Anderson, Walter Truett, ed. *The Truth about the Truth: De-confusing and Re-constructing the Postmodern World.* New York: G. P. Putman's Sons, 1995.

Anzaldúa, Gloria. *Borderlands: The New Mestiza/La Frontera.* San Francisco: Spinsters/Aunt Lute, 1987.

Apple, Michael W. "The Text and Cultural Politics." *Educational Researcher.* (October 1992): 4–19.

Ayers, William, et. al. *Teaching for Social Justice: A Democracy and Education Reader.* New York: Teachers College Press, 1998.

Banks, James A. *Educating Citizens in a Multicultural Society.* New York: Teachers College Press, 1997.

Banks, James, and Cherry McGee. *Handbook of Research on Multicultural Education.* New York: Macmillan, 1995.

Barber, Benjamin. "Public Schooling: Education for Democracy." In *The Public Purpose of Education and Schooling,* edited by John Goodlad and Timothy McMannon. San Francisco: Jossey-Bass, 1997.

Battistoni, Richard. *Public Schooling and Education of Democratic Citizens.* Jackson: University Press of Mississippi, 1988.

Battistoni, Richard, and William E. Hudson, eds. *Experiencing Citizenship: Concepts and Models for Service-Learning in Political Science.* Washington, D.C.: American Association of Higher Education, 1997.

Beezley, William H., Cheryl English Martin, and William E. French. "Introduction: Constructing Consent, Inciting Conflict." In *Rituals of Rule, Rituals of Resistance: Public Celebrations and Popular Culture in Mexico,* edited by William H. Beezley, Cheryl English Martin, and William E. French. Wilmington, Del.: Scholarly Resources, 1994.

Bellah Robert, et al. *Habits of the Heart.* New York: Harper & Row, 1985.

———. *The Good Society.* New York: Vintage, 1992.

Bhabha, Homi. "Narrating the Nation." In *Nationalism,* edited by John Hutchison and Anthony D. Smith. New York: Oxford University Press, 1994.

Billig, Michael. *Banal Nationalism.* Beverly Hills, Calif.: Sage Publications, 1995.

Bogardus, Emory S. *Essentials of Americanization.* Los Angeles: University of Southern California Press, 1923.

Bonilla, José María. *Evolución del Pueblo Mexicano.* 2nd ed. México: Herrero Hermanos, 1923. Quoted in Mary Kay Vaughn, *The State,*

Education, and Social Class in Mexico (1880–1928). DeKalb:
Northern Illinois University Press, 1982.

Bordieu, Pierre. *Outline of a Theory of Practice*, translated by Richard
Nice. Cambridge: Cambridge University Press, 1995.

Boyte, Harry, and Nancy Kari. *Building America: The Democratic
Promise of Public Work*. Philadelphia: Temple University Press, 1996.

Brice-Heath, Shirley. *Telling Tongues: Language Policy in Mexico,
Colony to Nation*. New York: Teachers College Press, 1972.

Burrell, Gibson, and Gareth Morgan. *Sociological Paradigms and
Organisational Analysis*. London: Heinemann, 1979.

Butler, Judith. *Bodies That Matter: On the Discursive Limits of Sex*.
New York: Routledge, 1993.

Calderón, Margarita. "Bilingual, Bicultural, and Binational
Cooperative Learning Communities for Students and Teachers."
Washington, D.C.: Educational Resources Information Center,
393 642, 1996.

Califa, Antonio J. "Declaring English the Official Language:
Prejudice Spoken Here." *Harvard Civil Liberties Law Review* 24
(1989): 293–348.

Calvo Pontón, Beatriz. *Educación Normal y Control Político*. México,
D. F.: Centro de Investigaciones y Estudios Superiores en
Antropología Social, 1989.

———. "The Policy of Modernization of Education: A Challenge to
Democracy in Mexico." In *Ethnic Identity and Power: Cultural
Contexts of Political Action in School and Society*, edited by Yali Zou
and Enrique T. Trueba. New York: State University of New York
Press, 1998.

Cherryholmes, Cleo H. "Social Knowledge and Citizenship
Education: Two Views of Truth and Criticism." *Curriculum Inquiry*
10 (1980): 115–41.

———. "U.S. Social and Political Education." *Teaching Political
Science* 8 (1981): 245–60.

———. *Power and Criticism Poststructural Investigations in Education*.
New York: Teachers College Press, 1988.

Christian, Donna. "Two-Way Bilingual Education: Students
    Learning through Two Languages." *Educational Practice Report* 12.
    Washington, D.C.: U.S. Department of Education, National
    Center for Research on Cultural Diversity and Second Language
    Learning, 1994.
Clifford, James. "Diaspora." *Cultural Anthropology* 9 (1994): 302–38.
Constance, Paul. "A Call to Action in the Classroom." *InterAmerican
    Development Bank (IDBAMERICA)* (March–April 1999): 22–23.
Crawford, James. "What Now for Bilingual Education?" *Rethinking
    Schools: An Urban Educational Journal* 13 (winter 1998/1999): 1, 4,
    5.
Dewey, John. *Experience and Education.* New York: Macmillan, 1938.
Dunn, Timothy J. *The Militarization of the U.S.–Mexico Border
    1978–1992: Low Intensity Conflict Doctrine Comes Home.* Austin:
    University of Texas Center for Mexican American Studies, 1996.
Edwards, John. "Monolingualism, Bilingualism, Multiculturalism,
    and Identity: Lessons from Recent Canadian Experience." In
    Monolingualism and Bilingualism: Lessons from Canada and Spain,
    edited by Sue Wright. Cleveland: Multilingual Matters, 1996.
El Paso Committee of the Border Project. "A Study of Conditions
    Affecting Children in El Paso County." El Paso: University of
    Texas at El Paso, 1948.
El Paso Independent School District. "Campus Profiles, 1997–98." El
    Paso: El Paso Independent School District, 1997–1998.
———. *Curriculum and Instruction, Bilingual Education.* El Paso: El
    Paso Independent School District, n.d.
Flores Balbuena, Gabriela. "Algunas reflexiones en torno al regimen
    juridico del sistema educativo nacional en México," unpublished
    paper, Ciudad Juárez, Chihuahua, Mexico, 1997.
Flores, Esteban T., et al. "Immigration Reform: An Analysis of
    Employer Sanctions." Washington, D.C.: Education Resources
    Information Center 323 074, 1990.
Foley, Douglas, E. *Learning Capitalist Culture: Deep in the Heart of
    Texas.* Philadelphia: University of Pennsylvania Press, 1990.

Foucault, Michel. *Discipline and Punish: The Birth of the Prison.* New York: Vintage Books, 1995.

Freire, Paulo. *Pedagogy of the Oppressed.* Rev. ed. New York: Continuum, 1996.

Fuchs, Lawrence. "The American Civic Culture and an Inclusivist Immigration Policy." In *Handbook of Multicultural Education.* edited by James Banks and Cherry McGee. New York: Macmillan, 1995.

Garcia, Mario. *Desert Immigrants.* New Haven, Conn.: Yale University Press, 1981.

Geertz, Clifford. *After the Fact: Two Countries, Four Decades, One Anthropologist.* Cambridge, Mass.: Harvard University Press, 1996.

Gutman, Amy. *Democratic Education.* Princeton, N.J.: Princeton University Press, 1987.

Hahn, Carole L. "Challenges to Civic Education in the United States." In *Civic Education across Countries, Twenty-four National Case Studies from the IEA Civic Education Project.* Amsterdam: International Association for the Evaluation of Educational Achievements, 1999.

Halstead, Mark J., and Monica J. Taylor, eds. *Values in Education and Education in Values.* London: Falmer Press, 1996.

Haney-López, Ian. *White by Law: The Legal Construction of Race.* New York: New York University Press, 1996.

Hartman, Edward George. *The Move to Americanize the Immigrant,* 2nd ed. New York: Columbia University Press, 1967.

Haugen, E. "Dialect, Language, and Nation." In *Sociolinguistics,* edited by J. B. Pride and Janet Holmes. London: Penguin Books, 1972.

Heath, Shirley. *Ways with Words: Language, Life and Work in Communities in Classrooms.* Cambridge: Cambridge University Press, 1983.

Heraldo de Chihuahua. "Se Integra a Internet la Escuela Porfirio Parra." *El Heraldo de Chihuahua,* December 11, 1996.

Hidalgo, Margarita. *Perceptions of Spanish-English Code-Switching in*

Juárez, Mexico. Albuquerque: University of New Mexico, Latin American Institute, 1988.

Hofstede, Geert. *Culture's Consequences: International Differences in Work-Related Values.* Beverly Hills, Calif.: Sage Publications, 1980.

Hymes, Dell. *Pidginization and Creolization of Languages.* Cambridge: Cambridge University Press, 1971.

Instituto de Investigación para el Desarrollo de la Educación, A.C. *Perfil de Formación de Maestros Primera Parte: Trayectoria y Prospectiva de la Modernización Educativa (1989–1994).* México, D.F.: Instituto de Proposiciones Estratégicas, A.C., 1992.

Instituto Nacional de Estadística Geografía e Informática. *Anuario Estadístico de Chihuahua.* Chihuahua: INEGI, 1998.

———. *Estadísticas Históricas de México, Tomo I.* México, D.F.: Instituto Nacional de Estadística Geografía e Informática, 1990.

Instituto Oaxaqueño de las Culturas. *Coloquio sobre derechos indígenas.* Oaxaca: Instituto Oaxaqueño de las Culturas, Fondo Estatal para la Culturea y las Artes, 1996.

Kelley, Robin. *Race Rebels: Culture, Politics, and the Black Working Class.* New York: Free Press, 1996.

Kohn, Alfie. *The Case against Standardized Testing: Raising the Scores, Ruining the Schools.* New York: Heinemann, 2000.

Langton, Kenneth, and M. Kent Jennings. "Political Socialization and the High School Civics Curriculum in the United States." *American Political Science Review* 62 (1968): 852–67.

Levinson, Bradley A., Douglas E. Foley, and Dorothy C. Holland, eds. *The Cultural Production of the Educated Person: Critical Ethnographies of Schooling and Local Practice.* Albany: State University of New York Press, 1996.

Litt, Edgar. "Civic Education, Community Norms, and Political Indoctrination." *American Journal of Sociology* 28 (February 1963): 69–75.

Márquez, Benjamin. *LULAC: The Evolution of a Mexican American Political Organization.* Austin: University of Texas Press, 1993.

Martínez Della Rocca, Salvador. *Estado, Educación y Hegemonía en México, 1920–1956.* México, D.F.: Editorial Línea, 1983.

Martínez, Oscar. *Border People: Life and Society in the U.S.–México Borderlands.* Tucson: University of Arizona Press, 1994.

Martusewicz, Rebecca A., and William M. Reynolds, eds. *Inside Out: Contemporary Critical Perspectives in Education.* New York: St. Martin's Press, 1994.

McCarthy Brown, Karen. *Mama Lola: A Vodou Priestess in Brooklyn.* Berkeley: University of California Press, 1991.

McLaren, Peter. "Unthinking Whiteness, Rethinking Democracy; a Farewell to the Blonde Beast; towards a Revolutionary Multiculturalism." *Educational Foundations* 29 (1997): 1–29.

———. *Life in Schools: An Introduction to Critical Pedagogy in the Foundations of Education.* 2nd ed. New York: Longman, 1994.

Merelman, Richard. "Democratic Politics and the Culture of American Education." *American Political Science Review* 74 (1980): 319–41.

Merriam, Sharan B. *Qualitative Research and Case Study Applications in Education.* San Francisco: Jossey-Bass Publishers, 1998.

Montejano, David. *Anglos and Mexicans in the Making of Texas 1836–1980.* Austin: University of Texas Press, 1987.

Morales-Gómez, Daniel A., and Carlos Alberto Torres. *The State, Corporatist Politics, and Educational Policy Making in Mexico.* New York: Praeger, 1990.

Nathan, Debbie. *Women and Other Aliens: Essays from the U.S.–Mexico Border.* El Paso: Cinco Puntos Press, 1987.

National Assessment of Educational Progress (NAEP). *1998 Civics Report Card* http://nced.ed.gov/nationsreportcard/, 1999.

National Commission on Civic Renewal. *A Nation of Spectators: How Civic Desengagement Weakens America and What We Can Do about It.* College Park, Md.: National Commission on Civic Renewal, n.d.

Nieto, Sonia. *Affirming Diversity: The Sociopolitical Context of Multicultural Education.* 2nd ed. New York: Longman, 1996.

Oakes Jeannie. *Keeping Track: How Schools Structure Inequality.* New Haven, Conn.: Yale University Press, 1985.

Ohanian, Susan. *One Size Fits Few: The Folly of Educational Standards.* Westport, Conn.: Heinemann, 1999.

Olneck, Michael. "Americanization and the Education of
    Immigrants, 1900–1925: An Analysis of Symbolic Action."
    American Journal of Education (August 1989): 398–423.

Ornelas, Carlos. *El sistema educativo Mexicano: La transición de fin de
    siglo.* México, D.F.: Centro de Investigación y Docencia
    Económica, 1995.

Orozco, Lorena. "Civic Education in the State of Morelos, Mexico."
    Master's thesis, University of Texas at El Paso, 1998.

Osuna, José Ángel Pescador. *Aportaciones para la Modernización
    Educativo.* México, D.F.: Universidad Pedagógica Nacional, 1989.

Pan, Phillip P. "For Some New to U.S. Schools, English Itself Is
    Biggest Test." *Washington Post,* September 7, 1999.

Pastor, Robert, and Jorge Castañeda. *Limits to Friendship: The United
    States and Mexico.* New York: Alfred A. Knopf, 1988.

Patton, Michael Quinn. *Qualitative Evaluation and Research Methods.*
    Newbury Park, Calif.: Sage Publications, 1990.

Paulston, Christina B. "Linguistic Consequences of Ethnicity and
    Nationalism in Multilingual Settings." In *Language and Education
    in Multilingual Settings,* edited by B. Spolsky. San Diego, Calif.:
    College Hill Press, 1986.

Paulston, Rolland G., ed. *Social Cartography: Mapping Ways of Seeing
    Social and Educational Change.* New York: Garland Publishing, 1996.

Peacock, James L. *The Anthropological Lens: Harsh Light, Soft Focus.*
    Cambridge: Cambridge University Press, 1986.

Phi Delta Kappan. *Values on Which We Agree.* Bloomington, Ind.: Phi
    Delta Kappan, 1996.

Pierce, Bessie. *Citizens' Organizations and the Civic Training of Youth.*
    New York: Scribner, 1933.

Pliego de Robles, Cecilia, and Luis Alberto Robles V. *Valores:
    Enseñanza activa de valores éticos.* Saltillo, México: Proyecto ETI-
    K, 1996.

Ponce de Leon, José María. *Anuario Estadístico del Estado de
    Chihuahua, Año 1910.* Chihuahua, Mexico: Sección de Estadística
    de la Secretaría de Gobierno, a cargo del Oficial Mayor C. José
    María Ponce de León, 1910.

Putnam, Robert, et al. "Bowling Alone: America's Declining Social Capital." *Journal of Democracy* 6 (1995): 1

———. *Bowling Alone: The Collapse and Revival of American Community.* New York: Simon & Schuster, 2000.

Raat, W. Dirk. *Mexico and the U.S.: Ambivalent Vistas.* 2nd ed. Athens: University of Georgia Press, 1996.

Ravitch, Diane. *National Standards in American Education.* Washington, D.C.: Brookings Institution Press, 1995.

Reeher, Grant, and Joseph Cammarano. *Education for Citizenship: Ideas and Innovations in Political Learning.* Lanham, Md.: Rowman & Littlefield, 1997.

Rendón, Laura I., Richard O. Hope, et al. *Educating a New Majority: Transforming America's Educational System for Diversity.* San Francisco: Jossey-Bass, 1996.

Rocha, Gregory G., and Robert H. Webking. *Politics and Public Education:* Edgewood v. Kirby *and the Reform of Public School Financing in Texas.* 2nd ed. Minneapolis: West Publishing, 1993.

Roett, Riordan, ed. *The Challenge of Intitutional Reform in Mexico.* Boulder, Colo.: Lynne Rienner, 1995.

Romo, Harriet, and Toni Falbo. *Latino High School Graduation.* Austin: University of Texas Press, 1996.

Rosaldo, Renato. *Culture and Truth.* Boston: Beacon Press, 1989.

Ruiz, Richard. "Orientations in Language Planning." *NABE: The Journal for the National Association for Bilingual Education* 8 (1984): 15–34.

Russell, Phillip. *Mexico in Transition.* Austin, Texas: Colorado River Press, 1977.

Salgado, Javier. "Awakenings in the Segundo Barrio: Mexican American Youth Association (MAYA) 1967–1972." M.A. Seminar Paper, University of Texas at El Paso, 1998.

Salinas de Gortari, Carlos. *The Educational Modernization Program, 1989–1994.* México, D.F.: Secretaría de Educación Pública, 1988.

San Miguel, Guadalupe. *Let Them All Take Heed: Mexican Americans and the Campaign for Educational Equity in Texas, 1910–1981.* Austin: University of Texas Press, 1987.

Scheurich, James Joseph, and Michelle D. Young. "Coloring
    Epistemologies: Are Our Research Epistemologies Racially
    Biased?" *Educational Researcher* 26 (1997): 4–16.

Schmelkes, Sylvia. "The Problems of the Decentralization of
    Education: A View from Mexico." In *Latin American Education:
    Comparative Perspectives,* edited by Carlos Alberto Torres and
    Adriana Puiggros. Boulder, Colo.: Westview, 1997.

Scott, James C. *Domination and the Arts of Resistance: Hidden
    Transcripts.* New Haven, Conn.: Yale University Press, 1990.

Secretaría de Educación Pública. *Los Libros de Texto Gratuitos y las
    Correientes del Pensamiento Nacional, Vol. II.* México, D.F.:
    Biblioteca del Consejo Nacional Técnico de la Educación, 1962.

———. *Libro integrado, Segundo grado.* México, D.F.: Comisión
    Nacional de los Libros de Texto Gratuitos, 1966.

———. *¿Ha fracasado el indigenismo?: Reportaje de una conrtroversia.*
    México, D.F.: Secretaría de Educación Pública, 1971.

———. *Artículo 3 Constitucional y Ley General de Educación.* México,
    D.F.: Secretaría de Educación Pública, 1993.

———. *Bats'i K'op, Lengua Tsotsil, Chiapas, primer ciclo.* México, D.F.:
    Comisión Nacional de los Libros de Texto Gratuitos, 1994.

———. *Educación Básica: Secundaria Plan y Programas de Estudio,
    1993.* México D.F.: Secretaria de Educación Pública, 1993.

———. *Historia, Cuarto Grado.* México, D.F.: Comisión de los
    Libros de Texto Gratuitos, 1996.

Sharp, John. *Bordering the Future: Challenge and Opportunity in the
    Texas Border Regions.* Austin: Texas Comptroller of Public
    Accounts, 1998.

Sherman, John W. *The Mexican Right: The End of Revolutionary
    Reform, 1929–1940.* Westport, Conn.: Praeger, 1997.

Shirley, Dennis. *Community Organizing for Urban School Reform.*
    Austin: University of Texas Press, 1997.

Sigel, Roberta, ed. *Learning about Politics: A Reader in Political
    Socialization.* New York: Random House, 1970.

Singer, Mark. "I Pledge Allegiance: A Liberal Town's School System

Meets the New Patriotism." *New Yorker,* November 26, 2001, 54–61.

Solana, Fernando, Raúl Cardiel Reyes, and Raúl Bolaños Martínez. *Historia de la Educación en México.* México, D.F.: Secretaría de Educación Pública, 1981.

Spener, David, and Kathleen Staudt, eds. *The U.S.–Mexico Border: Transcending Divisions and Contesting Identities.* Boulder, Colo.: Lynne Rienner, 1998.

Spindler, George, ed. *Education and Cultural Process: Anthropological Approaches.* Prospect Heights, Ill.: Waveland Press, 1987.

Spring, Joel. *American Education: An Introduction to Social and Political Aspects.* 5th ed. New York: Longman, 1991.

———. *Conflict of Interests: The Politics of American Education.* 3rd ed. Boston: McGraw Hill, 1995.

Stafford-López, Gloria. *A Place in El Paso.* Albuquerque: University of New Mexico Press, 1996.

Star, Susan Leigh. "The Sociology of the Invisible." In *Social Organization and Social Process: Essays in Honor of Anselm Strauss,* edited by D. R. Maines. New York: Aldine de Gruyter, 1991.

Staudt, Kathleen. *Policy, Politics, and Gender: Women Gaining Ground.* West Hartford, Conn.: Kumarian Press, 1998.

———. *Free Trade? Informal Economies at the U.S.–Mexico Border.* Philadelphia: Temple University Press, 1998.

———. "Democracy Education for More than the Few." In *Developing Democratic Character in the Young,* edited by Roger Soder et al. San Francisco: Jossey-Bass, 2001.

Staudt, Kathleen, and Randy Capps, "Con La Ayuda de Dios? El Pasoans Manage the 1996 Immigration and Welfare Reforms." In *Living in the Interim: Immigrant Communities and Welfare "Reform" in North America,* edited by Ana Aparicio, Phil Kretsedmas, and Kalyani Rai. Westport, Conn.: Greenwood, forthcoming.

Staudt, Kathleen, and David Spener. "The View from the Frontier: Theoretical Perspectives Undisciplined." In *The U.S.–Mèxico Border: Transcending Divisions, Contesting Identities,* edited by

David Spener and Kathleen Staudt. Boulder, Colo.: Lynne
      Rienner, 1998.

Still, Rae Files. *The Gilmer–Aikin Bills: A Study in the Legislative
      Process.* Austin: The Steck Company, 1950.

Stromquist, Nellie. *Women in Education in Latin America.* Boulder,
      Colo.: Lynne Rienner, 1992.

Terrazas, Ana Cecilia. "Comercializan el Himno Nacional." *Diario de
      Juárez*, December 28, 1997, 6A.

Tobin, Joseph, David Wu, and Dana Davidson. *Preschool in Three
      Cultures.* New Haven, Conn.: Yale University Press, 1989.

Tocqueville, Alexis de. *Democracy in America,* translated by Henry
      Reeve. New York: Oxford University Press, 1947.

Tolo, Kenneth. *The Civic Education of American Youth: From State
      Policies to School District Practices.* Policy Research Project Report
      #133. Austin: LBJ School of Public Affairs, University of Texas,
      1999.

Torney-Purta, Judith, et al. *Civic Education across Countries: Twenty-
      four National Case Studies from the IEA Civic Education Project.*
      Amsterdam: International Association for the Evaluation of
      Educational Achievement, 1999.

Torres, Carlos Alberto. "Democracy, Education, and
      Multiculturalism: Dilemmas of Citizenship in a Global World."
      Comparative Education Review 42 (1998): 421–47.

Trejo, Guillermo. "The Politics of Educational Reform in Mexico:
      Ambivalence toward Change." In *The Challenge of Institutional
      Reform in Mexico,* edited by Riordan Roett. Boulder, Colo.: Lynne
      Rienner, 1995.

Triandis, Harry. "Crosscultural Industrial and Organizational
      Psychology." In *Handbook of Industrial and Organizational
      Psychology*, edited by Harry Triandis et al. Palo Alto, Calif.:
      Consulting Psychologists, 1994.

Trochin, William. "The Knowledge Base: On-line Research Methods
      Textbook." www.trochin.human.cornell.edu, 1997.

Trueba, Henry. "Healing Multicultural America: Mexican

Immigrants Rise to Power." In *Rural America*. Washington, D.C.: Falmer Press, 1993.

United Nations Development Programme. *Human Development Report 1996*. New York: Oxford University Press, 1996.

United Nations Educational, Scientific and Cultural Orgnization. *The State of Education 1995*. New York: Oxford University Press, 1996.

United Nations Research Institute for Social Development. *States in Disarray*. Geneva: United Nations Research Institute for Social Development, 1995.

U.S. Commission on Civil Rights. *The Mexican American Education Study*. Vols. 1–6. Washington, D.C.: U.S. Commission on Civil Rights, 1971–1974.

U.S. Commission on Immigration Reform. *Becoming an American: Immigration and Immigrant Policy: A Report to Congress*. Washington, D.C.: U.S. Commission on Immigration Reform, 1977.

U.S. Department of Labor. *Futurework: Trends and Challenges for Work in the 21st Century*. Washington, D.C.: U.S. Department of Labor, 1999.

U.S. National Commission on Excellence in Education. *A Nation at Risk: The Imperative for Educational Reform*. Washington, D.C.: U.S. National Commission on Excellence in Education, 1983.

Urciuoli, Bonnie. "Language and Borders." *Annual Review of Anthropology* 24 (1995): 525–46.

Valdés, Guadalupe. "The World Outside and Inside Schools: Language and Immigrant Children." *Educational Researcher* 27 (1998): 4–18.

Vaughan, Mary K. *Cultural Politics in Revolution: Teachers, Peasants, and Schools in* Mexico, 1930–1940. Arizona: University of Arizona Press, 1997.

———. *The State Education, and Social Class in Mexico (1880–1928)* DeKalb: Northern Illinois University Press, 1982.

Vélez-Ibáñez, Carlos. *Border Visions*. Tucson: University of Arizona Press, 1996.

Verba, Sidney, Kay Schlozman, and Henry Brady. *Voice and Equality: Civic Volunteerism in American Politics.* Cambridge, Mass.: Harvard University Press, 1995.

Vila, Pablo Sergio. "Everyday Life, Culture and Identity on the Mexican-American Border: The Ciudad Juárez-El Paso Case." Ph.D. diss., University of Texas at Austin, 1994.

Ward, Peter, and Victoria Rodríguez, with Enrique Cabrero Mendoza. "Education." In *New Federalism and State Government in Mexico,* Austin: LBJ School of Public Affairs, University of Texas, 1999.

Weber, David. *Foreigners in Their Native Land.* Albuquerque: University of New Mexico Press, 1973.

Wheatley, Meg. *Leadership and the New Science: Learning about Organization from an Orderly Universe.* San Francisco: Berrett-Koehler Publishers, 1992.

Wiggin, Gladys A. *Education and Nationalism: An Historical Interpretation of American Education.* New York: McGraw Hill, 1962.

Wink, Joan. *Critical Pedagogy: Notes from the Real World.* New York: Longman, 1997.

Wolcott, Harry F. *Transforming Qualitative Data: Description, Analysis, and Interpretation.* Thousand Oaks, Calif.: Sage Publications, 1994.

———. *The Art of Fieldwork.* Walnut Creek, Calif.: AltaMira Press, 1995.

Wright, Sue. *Monolingualism and Bilingualism: Lessons from Canada and Spain.* Cleveland: Multilingual Matters, 1996.

www.fairtest.org

www.inegi.gob.mx

www.rethinkingschools.org

www.sep.gob.mx

www.tea.state.tx.us

Yzaguirre, Raul "What's the Fuss? Rethinking Schools." *An Urban Educational Journal* 13, no. 2 (winter 1998–99): 8.

INDEX